BACKROADS & BYWAYS OF
VIRGINIA

BACKROADS & BYWAYS OF
VIRGINIA

Drives, Daytrips
& Weekend Excursions

Bill Lohmann

The Countryman Press
Woodstock, Vermont

ISBN 978-0-88150-904-5

Book design by Hespenheide Design
Map by Paul Woodward, © The Countryman Press
Interior photos by the author unless otherwise specified
Composition by Eugenie Delaney

Published by The Countryman Press, P.O. Box 748, Woodstock, VT 05091

Distributed by W. W. Norton & Company, Inc., 500 Fifth Avenue, New York, NY 10110

Printed in the United States of America

10 9 8 7 6 5

To my family

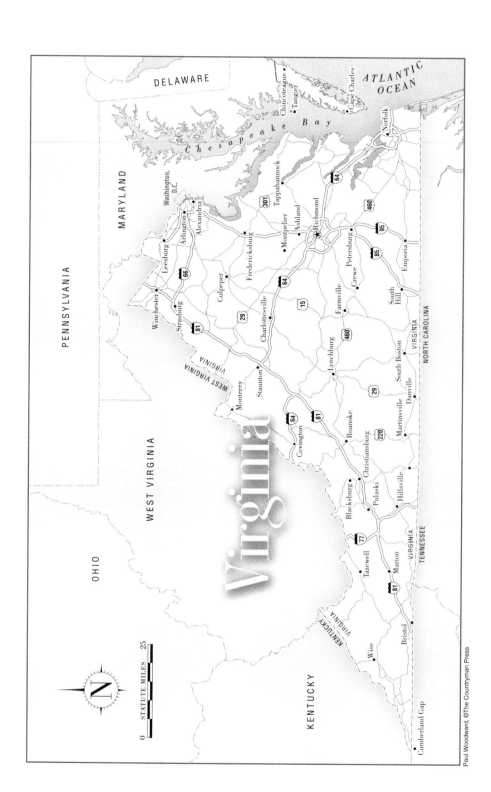

Contents

Acknowledgments

Putting together this book was far from a solitary endeavor. Over the months I spent traveling around the state gathering material, I needed the assistance and kindness of many. There aren't enough pages to list everyone who lent a helping hand, but I'd like to thank a few people in particular:

Tom Baker, Pete and Mary Calos, Sibella Giorello, Neil and Susan Kaye, Greg and Deborah Morse, Matthew O'Quinn, Bob Rittenhouse, Felecia Shelor, Mike and Jann Steele, Tamra Talmadge-Anderson, Mike and Yvonne Thompson, Gary Waugh, Charlotte Whitted, and my good friend and colleague Bob Brown. The editors I worked most closely with on this project—Kim Grant and Sandy Rodgers—for their keen eyes, guidance, and much-appreciated encouragement.

And, of course, I offer special appreciation for my family, who not only scribbled notes as I drove so we didn't run off the road, but also provided boundless supplies of patience and support:

My daughter, Melissa, the college senior, who greeted me every morning with, "What chapter are you on?"

My daughter, Alexandra, an avid reader and budding writer, who accompanied me on several road trips and discovered her new favorite place in the world, the Green Valley Book Fair in Mt. Crawford.

My son, Jack, who also rode along on a number of adventures, including a long, musical jaunt along the Crooked Road through Southwest Virginia. A highlight of that trip for Jack, a violinist, was our lunch with Jack and Nannie Branch at their home outside Bristol, after which my Jack joined Jack Branch, an excellent fiddler and an even better violin maker, for a mini-jam session. Their duet of "Amazing Grace" was one of the best moments of this entire experience.

And my wife, Robin, who cheerfully took over a lot of my share of the household duties while I was doing a poor impersonation of someone trying to hold down two writing jobs, and, who, at one point, asked, "Have you grown roots yet?" as I sat for endless hours at the kitchen table, sifting through notes and typing on my laptop.

I've finally pushed myself away from the table, and I've checked for roots.

Not yet.

Thank you all.

Introduction

This is how you really get to know Virginia: As you drive down US 13, the main thoroughfare for the length of the Eastern Shore, pull over at a farmers' market and buy a bag of sweet potatoes, tomatoes, or some other freshly harvested specialty. Linger and chat. Find out where you can get the best crab cakes or the tastiest clam fritters. Follow the advice.

Clear across the state, in the far southwestern corner, drive the Crooked Road—as the name suggests, a twisting ribbon of pavement that curls through the mountains—where old-time music comes alive at country stores, in cozy theaters, and on street corners outside music shops. Don't forget your guitar.

Interstate highways can carry you through Virginia, but only the back roads will bring the state to you. I know this from personal experience. I was born and raised in Virginia, and I've lived here for most of my adult life, but it wasn't until I started venturing into the hinterlands of the commonwealth that I truly started appreciating—and knowing—the state. I always knew, naturally, that from my home in the middle of the state I was no more than two hours from the beach and an hour from the mountains. But who knew what gems shined beyond my view off two-lane roads on the Eastern Shore or deep in the hills of the remote southwestern corner of the state?

My job as a columnist and feature writer for the *Richmond Times-Dispatch* has taken me all over Virginia, from the uninhabited barrier islands off the coast to deep into the western mountains. Everywhere I've gone, the people have been hospitable and their stories rich, whether they're knee-deep in creek water digging clams or they're sitting at the counter waiting on breakfast at the Hillsville Diner.

Over the years, I've traveled thousands of miles of roadways in Virginia—most of them paved—and I've filled hundreds of reporters' notebooks, all of which has led me to this conclusion: the state offers something for everyone.

Virginia, of course, is steeped in history. You can cover almost 200 years of American history in a matter of a few hours and 23 miles. Start at Jamestown, the site of the first permanent English settlement in the New World, move on to Colonial Williamsburg, and then to Yorktown, where the British surrendered to end the Revolutionary War.

History reaches all over the state. Stroll through the place George Washington *really* slept at Mt. Vernon, his estate and working farm on the Potomac River. Witness up close the genius of Thomas Jefferson at Monticello. But they are not alone. Six other U.S. presidents were born in Virginia, and most of their homes are open, too, including James Madison's Montpelier, James Monroe's Ash Lawn, William Henry Harrison's Berkeley Plantation, John Tyler's Sherwood Forest, and Woodrow Wilson's Manse.

Walk at dawn, as I have, Manassas National Battlefield, site of two great Civil War battles including the war's first major land battle, and stand at the muscular statue of Confederate General Thomas "Stonewall" Jackson. But don't stop at Manassas. Virginia brims with Civil War battlefields, stretching the width of the state and the length of the war, all the way to Appomattox, where Lee surrendered to Grant.

The Blue Ridge Parkway and Skyline Drive are two of the prettiest drives anywhere, particularly in the fall when the leaves start to turn and the mountains are awash in color. Follow the old Valley Turnpike, US 11, the route taken by immigrants streaming into the Shenandoah Valley in the 17th and 18th centuries. Or, if you have the time, take a trip on US 58, the state's longest road. Spread a blanket on the sand at Virginia Beach and watch the sun rise, then drive more than 500 miles westward and see the sun set at Cumberland Gap, the famed mountain passage that was young America's first gateway to the West. The same feet that stood in the Atlantic surf can straddle the Virginia-Kentucky border at a stripe painted on the walkway at the Gap.

Wherever you go, don't be in a hurry. Linger over a second cup of coffee at a friendly diner or on the porch of a cabin tucked in the mist-covered hills near the Blue Ridge Parkway. Sip a glass of wine at one of the state's 140 wineries, a mug of beer at numerous micro-breweries, or a taste of cider at Albemarle Ciderworks in North Garden near Charlottesville, or Foggy Ridge Cider in Dugspur, in the southwest part of the state. If you're feeling real adventurous, you can drop by Belmont Farm Distillery in Culpeper and watch *legal* moonshine being made. Liquor laws prevent sampling the corn whiskey on site, but at liquor stores and online you can purchase Virginia Lightning, made in a genuine solid copper-pot still. .

Don't just drive. Get out, look around, breathe in the fresh air. Hike if you like. More than 500 miles of the Appalachian Trail—roughly a quarter of America's most famous walking path—unfurl through Virginia's mountains with easy access points for day or weekend expeditions. You can hike to the top of Mt. Rogers, which is the highest peak in Virginia and just up a spur trail from the Appalachian Trail, or you can walk a couple of miles of the A. T. on more level terrain, enjoy a picnic, and get back in the car. But think how cool it will be to drop this line at your next cocktail party: "Well, yes, I've hiked the A. T."

Take your bicycle along. There are numerous rails-to-trails, multipurpose paths on converted rail beds, that are perfect for biking: Virginia Creeper Trail and New River Trail State Park, both in Southwest Virginia, are two.

There are festivals galore from spring through fall. On US 58 alone, you can hit the Peanut Festival in Suffolk, the Pork Festival in Emporia, the Cantaloupe Festival near South Boston (ever try a big scoop of vanilla ice cream in a halved cantaloupe the size of a small watermelon?), the Peach Festival in Stuart, and, of all things, the Cabbage Festival in Vesta.

You can pick apples, peaches, or berries in season at any number of pick-your-own orchards and farms, shop for antiques, lie on your back in an open field on a starry night and connect the dots of constellations, and, well, you get the idea. If you can think it, you can probably find it on the back roads of Virginia.

I drove about 6,000 miles over six months to gather material for this book. Many of the places I'd visited before; some I hadn't. I certainly couldn't get to every place I wanted or that deserved to be included; this book is not meant to be exhaustive, but to include some places you might want to visit on a day or weekend drive. I made good use of a GPS device to help me find my way, but I still always take my dog-eared Virginia State Road Atlas, which offers pages of detailed maps and an index of localities and points of interest all over the state. I've found my way around some of the most remote roads using this atlas, which I've come to refer to as The Magic Map.

Other advice: Purchase annual passes from the National Park Service and Virginia State Parks. Prices are modest and pay for themselves with visits to only a few parks or historic sites. The state park system, by the way, is remarkable in its variety and quality, with 35 parks scattered across the commonwealth. (http://www.dcr.virginia.gov/state_parks/index.shtml) Make use of the terrific Internet resources of the various places you might want to visit around Virginia. A great starting place is the state's official tourism web site: http://www.virginia.org.

My travels dramatically illustrated how close to the edge that restaurants, shops, and other businesses in small towns and rural areas exist and how devastating a sour economy can be on those family-run operations. I found restaurants that I remembered as thriving only a few years earlier sporting new names or new owners or, sadly, boarded up with no evidence of earlier success. This is another way of saying that information contained in any travel book can change in a hurry for any number of reasons.

Yet, I've also found the people who live far from the major thoroughfares are, by necessity, a resilient bunch. They've battled for years against vanishing industries and dwindling populations, highway bypasses, and, in some cases, encroaching development, trying to maintain the way of life their families may have known for generations. Meeting people like that is enlightening and enriching and a lesson in perspective.

Working on a six-month series of stories about US 58 some years ago, *Times-Dispatch* photographer Bob Brown and I started at Virginia Beach and worked our way across the state, story by story and week by week, until we reached Cumberland Gap. We were proud of ourselves for the way we'd organized our journey until someone at the Gap, good-naturedly, told us: "You started at the wrong end."

Like everything else, it all depends on your point of view.

Every place has something to offer, but not every one has what might be considered a full-blown tourism industry with amusement parks or museums or bright, flashing lights. After touring a cave at Cumberland Gap National Historical Park, I was talking to Lucas Wilder, one of the young park rangers who led the delightful tour. He was born and raised down the road from the park, in a small community along US 58 called Ewing, and I could tell he loves the place. I asked him what there is for tourists to do around there. He was almost apologetic in saying, not much.

"That's a good thing," he said, "and a bad thing."

No, I said, thinking of the sheer beauty and tranquility of the valley along that stretch of road, that's a good thing.

CHAPTER

1

A Shore Thing

Known for wild ponies, the Eastern Shore is much more

Estimated length: 75 miles
Estimated time: 2 days

Getting there: From Virginia Beach, head north on US 13 across the Chesapeake Bay Bridge-Tunnel.

Highlights: The wild ponies of **Chincoteague**–remember Misty?—made the **Eastern Shore** famous. However, a leisurely drive along US 13, the Shore's main artery, reveals this fertile agricultural peninsula wedged between the **Atlantic Ocean** and the **Chesapeake Bay** has much more to offer: charming small towns such as **Onancock**, its natural coastline, fresh seafood, and boutique wineries. Even motoring across the **Chesapeake Bay Bridge-Tunnel** is an event.

Dubbed an "engineering wonder of the world," the Chesapeake Bay Bridge-Tunnel earns its praise, but it probably won't take your breath away—unless you have a phobia about driving over open water, or under it. The bridge-tunnel stretches more than 17 miles across the mouth of the Chesapeake Bay, from Virginia Beach to the southern tip of the Eastern

LEFT: The light of Assateague Lighthouse, on the Eastern Shore's Assateague Island, can be seen almost 20 miles out to sea.

Shore, and includes two mile-long tunnels that allow ships to sail in and out of the busy Port of Hampton Roads. As long as the weather's good and traffic is moving, driving across the bridge-tunnel takes less than a half-hour, a vast improvement over the ferry system that was in place before the bridge-tunnel opened in 1964.

We leave the mainland behind, exiting I-64 onto US 13, which carries us to the bridge-tunnel toll plaza. The one-way toll is $12, but the return trip is only $5 if you make it within 24 hours of your original crossing and you hang on to the receipt. At 3.5 miles into the crossing, we stop and park on Sea Gull Island, the southernmost of the span's four man-made islands that, as you're heading toward the Shore, comes just before entering the first tunnel. The island has a restaurant, gift shop, and a 625-foot fishing pier that provides the rare opportunity for deep-sea fishing—the bay's depth runs 25 to 100 feet along the path of the bridge-tunnel—without a boat.

We walk around, appreciative of the view, watching ships pass through the shipping channel preserved by the tunnel. Small fishing boats bob on the bay near the island's foundation of giant rocks, a haven for schools of fish. In the gift shop, we browse among postcards, T-shirts, and assorted souvenirs, then peek in the restaurant where the menu includes crab, shrimp, and other seafood. Back outside, we stroll down the pier, crowded with locals and tourists camped out with coolers and lawn chairs, as they fish for bluefish, trout, croaker, flounder, and even sharks and stingrays. There's no charge to fish and a fishing license is not required, but fishermen and fisherwomen must pay the same toll as everyone else to get here.

"In many cases, we have folks who come to Virginia Beach or to the Hampton Roads area and actually take a morning or an afternoon just for the purpose of crossing, doing a U-turn . . . and going back across," says Jeffrey B. Holland, executive director of the bridge-tunnel. "It is a place to visit. But our primary mission is to provide the safest passage that we can for all traveling customers regardless of purpose."

Back in the car, we continue our ride across the bridge-tunnel. Once on the Shore, a new Eastern Shore Welcome Center, on the east side of US 13, is a good place to load up on brochures and become acclimated to what's available on the Shore. Just beyond that is another visitor center, for the Eastern Shore of Virginia National Wildlife Refuge, that's tucked away and takes a little effort to find, but is worth the trouble. Just head east on Seaside Road and wend your way a short distance to the facility.

The refuge consists of more than 1,200 acres on the southern end of the Shore, set aside for protection largely because it's considered one of the most important migratory bird concentration points along the East Coast. In the fall, millions of birds and butterflies rest in the refuge until favorable winds help them cross the bay as they head south for the winter. The visitor center offers interactive exhibits, wildlife observation platforms, and walking trails.

While on the Shore, don't forget the home-grown wines. As you motor along US 13, you have a choice of three wineries: **Bloxom Vineyards** in Bloxom, **Chatham Vineyards** in Machipongo, and **Holly Grove Vineyards** in Franktown. All offer tours and tastings.

I've visited Chatham Vineyards and Winery on a couple of occasions to sample the wines and talk to John Wehner, who operates the place with his wife, Mills, and their three children.

"The Eastern Shore is a wonderful climate for growing wine grapes," says Wehner. "It's a moderate maritime climate with a nice breeze from the bay or from the ocean, and nice, long Indian summers."

If you like a little activity with your wine, Chatham Vineyards, in conjunction with SouthEast Expeditions, offers wine-kayak tours that feature paddling and sightseeing as well as stops to enjoy bottles of Chardonnay, Rosé, or Merlot.

"It's a great way to see some of the creeks off the bay," Wehner says. "You get a lot of eagles here. You see cranes, blue heron, snowy egrets. People are able to come here on a private farm, get a little exercise, and see the nature the Shore has to provide."

We return to US 13 and go north about 3 miles to VA 704, where we turn to the west and follow the signs to Kiptopeke State Park on the bay side of the Shore. Named for an Indian who acted kindly toward early white settlers, Kiptopeke means "big water." The park, the former site of an old ferry landing, offers swimming, fishing, and boating, as well as walking trails, some connected by wooden boardwalks. We spend the late afternoon strolling on a woodland trail. We come to a steep wooden staircase, a substantial, low-hanging tree climb looming across it. Thump! I saw it coming but still manage to experience it headfirst. I highly recommend ducking.

Kiptopeke State Park, on the bay side of the Eastern Shore, is a popular place for swimming, fishing, boating, and biking.

Kiptopeke has a campground and cabins, but we already have a place for the night, just up the road in Cape Charles. First, though, we have dinner on our minds. We have a number of choices, none run-of-the-mill, roadside restaurants.

Sting-Ray's features fresh local seafood—and gas. Yes, it's at an Exxon Station on US 13, about 9 miles north of the bridge-tunnel. Order at the counter, take a seat, and your steamed crabs or soft-shell crab platter or whatever will be brought to you. The place has a good reputation and a nickname: Chez Exxon.

A couple of miles west of US 13 is Cape Charles, a bay town in the midst of a revival. Some of its fine old houses have been restored; others remain vacant and for sale. A few have been transformed into bed-and-breakfast inns. If you're hungry, Mason Avenue, the main business strip, offers a number of good options, including Kelly's Gingernut Pub, in a former bank building. I've enjoyed Kelly's in the past, but on this night I want to try something different, so we head for J. H. West Seafood at the recommendation of local friends. From Kiptopeke State Park, go north on

US 13 and then west on Townsend Drive. You'll see it just ahead: a small, plain cinderblock building. Nothing fancy outside or in. It's a seafood market with a few tables. No fine china or linen tablecloths, but a lot of fresh seafood in the display cases. I order the daily special, a sampler of fried shrimp, scallops, and oysters that comes with collard greens, baked potato, and sweet iced tea. Excellent.

After dinner, we drive north toward Cape Charles to Rittenhouse Motor Lodge, an old-style motor court hidden among a grove of pines and a thicket of azaleas on the side of US 13. Guests park their vehicles just a few feet from the doors to their rooms that are clean and comfortable but have no phones or hot tubs. If you're looking for a five-star hotel, this is not for you. However, if you're looking for a nice, quiet place where you can sit in a lawn chair outside your room and listen to songbirds and breathe in the fragrant scent of gardenias, then give it a shot.

Bob Rittenhouse opened his motel in the 1950s. His father, a lumberman, cut the wood; his mother helped him clear the land with an ax and a hatchet. He's still at it: still doing the laundry, still watering the plants, still sitting on the motel's front porch cheerfully chatting late into the night with guests and neighbors. He lives in an apartment just behind the office, as he has since the early 1950s.

"I get the nicest people," says the 81-year-old Rittenhouse, as we sit and chat on the porch. "Almost all of my guests become friends. I get them from everywhere: Europe, South America, China. It's magical, I tell you, totally magical."

The traffic whizzes past on US 13. We can hear it, but barely see it. The appeal of the Shore, Rittenhouse says, is subtle.

The water tower built to resemble a lighthouse welcomes visitors to Cape Charles, at one time a busy railroad town.

"You have to take your time, sit down and talk to somebody," says Rittenhouse, who was born and raised here. "We're not a big production. I think the world is not geared for the Shore, but I think the Shore is delightful."

The next morning, we say goodbye to Rittenhouse and head for another landmark, the Exmore Diner, a converted railcar that first opened as a restaurant in 1954. The diner, 20 miles north of Cape Charles in Exmore on US 13-Business, is one of the most popular restaurants on the Shore, and I quickly see why as we settle into a booth. The service is fast and friendly, and meals are reasonably priced. An omelet and home fries set me back less than $6. Just a cool place to eat.

Now, we have a decision to make: There is much to see, but our time

Misty, the wild pony who made Chincoteague famous, is memorialized on the town's main street.

If you have the time, rent, borrow, or buy a kayak or canoe and paddle around the creeks and inlets that help make the Shore such an intriguing place. Better yet, arrange a guided tour.

In fact, you'd be foolish to visit the undeveloped seaside barrier islands of the Shore without the assistance of a local guide, such as Rick Kellam. The islands are not far offshore, but changing ocean tides make reaching them through the salt marshes and tidal mudflats tricky and even dangerous. Once there, though, you will be astounded by their beauty, and their desolation.

"One of the last great places on Earth left in its natural form and not screwed up by man," Kellam tells me. "Yet."

The Nature Conservancy owns and protects most of the 23 islands, describing this stretch as "the longest expanse of coastal wilderness remaining on the Eastern Seaboard."

Kellam, who's worked as a waterman and as an officer with the Virginia State Marine Police, operates **Broadwater Bay EcoTours**. On a previous trip, he took me to **Cedar Island**, steering his 24-foot skiff through 2 miles of marshes to reach the deserted island, inhabited by no other humans but covered with whelk shells.

Dave Burden of **SouthEast Expeditions** also leads tours, including kayaking excursions of favorite clamming spots in bayside creeks that probably don't look a whole lot different than when Captain John Smith explored here in 1608. Burden is not a Shore native, but he might as well be. He moved here in the late 1990s, and can't imagine leaving. I once spent an afternoon with Burden, gathering and steaming a basket of littleneck clams. We sat on a dock, dipping the clams in chardonnay from a local winery.

"Definitely," says Burden, "the best part of my job."

is limited. Our priority, though, is getting to Chincoteague, where we can look for the wild ponies, which is the reason my 15-year-old daughter wanted to come with me. She remains a big fan of *Misty of Chincoteague*, the 1947 classic by Marguerite Henry.

On the way, we visit Onancock, a picturesque town with a lot going for it. Just 15 miles to the north of Exmore and on the bay side, Onancock has art galleries, an old-time movie theater, a gourmet coffee shop, a wine bar, a boutique hotel and restaurant, and numerous fun, quirky shops. At a favorite of mine, the House of Deals on Market Street, you can find a little of everything. A Ford Model-T showroom in its earlier life, the ostensible hardware store has obscure tools, but also fresh clams, bicycles, sweet potatoes, nightcrawlers, and, if you look hard enough, cans of evaporated milk.

"Most of the time if you need something and can't find it," says a clerk I speak to, "you can probably find it in here."

Over at gardenArt on King Street, a funky garden shop in the town's old power plant, customers are welcome to bring their pooches for monthly Yappy Hours. It's that kind of town.

Back to US 13, we point the car toward Chincoteague, just a few miles south of the Maryland border. An easy drive, US 13 is mostly four lanes with occasional traffic lights. Fields of corn, cotton, and tomatoes line the road. Vegetable stands sprout in warm weather, and it's not unusual to see farmers parked on the side of the road, their beds filled with watermelons or bushel baskets of Hyman sweet potatoes, the white-fleshed beauties that are a specialty on the Shore.

From Onancock, Chincoteague is another 20 miles north on US 13 and then 10 miles east on VA 175 toward the ocean. Before Chincoteague, though, we encounter the giant satellite dishes and tall fences that signal we have reached NASA's Wallops Flight Facility. No rocket launches are scheduled, but we stop at the visitor center, which is on the right side of VA 175 as we drive toward Chincoteague. Admission is free to the center, which features exhibits related to Wallops' projects. Plus, you can have your picture taken with a rocket.

The most touristy of the Shore's towns, Chincoteague is actually an island that serves as a gateway to Assateague Island National Seashore. If dining or shopping is your wish, Chincoteague can fulfill that with a number of shops and restaurants. You also can play miniature golf to your heart's content. Traffic can be congested on busy summer days, but it's not impossible to navigate. The town has plenty of lodging, too.

Our mission, though, is the national seashore and, within it, the Chincoteague National Wildlife Refuge. That's where the ponies live. From the main road, we see the ponies—from a distance—roaming through the vast expanses of wild grasses. We also spy them from an observation deck we reach following an easy mile-long walk through a pine forest. Less easy are the 198 steps up to the top of the red-and-white-striped Assateague Island Lighthouse. Hoof it up and enjoy the magnificent view of the surrounding islands and salt marshes.

The long stretch of beach at Assateague Island National Seashore beckons visitors to the ocean.

Hike and bike your way around the park, or simply drive as we do to the end of the road, which brings us to one of the prettiest beaches you'll ever want to see. The park contains miles and miles of pristine beach. On summer weekends, the crowds are thick and parking is a challenge, but it's worth dipping your toes—or more—in the Atlantic.

For a late lunch, we leave the park, cross the causeway and return to the traffic circle re-entering the town of Chincoteague and park between Woody's Beach Barbecue and Woody's Fried Chicken Joint, a couple of trailers that share a parking lot, a beach motif, and terrific food. I favor the barbecue trailer from a previous trip, being fond of The Memphis, a pulled pork sandwich smothered with cole slaw and red barbecue sauce. The proprietor cooks the meat in a smoker behind the trailer. The rest of the food is homemade, too.

After a quick stop for an ice cream cone, we head for home, back down US 13 and a return trip across the Chesapeake Bay Bridge-Tunnel. I reach for my wallet to make sure I still have the receipt from the previous day's crossing.

IN THE AREA

Accommodations

Bayview Waterfront, 35350 Copes Drive, Belle Haven. Call 757-442-6963. Bed-and-breakfast inn overlooking Occohannock Creek and the Chesapeake Bay beyond. Web site: http://www.bayviewwaterfrontbedand breakfast.com.

Cape Charles House, 645 Tazewell Avenue, Cape Charles. Call 757-331-4920. The Colonial Revival house is one of the largest in town with a wraparound porch. Web site: http://www.capecharleshouse.com.

Charlotte Hotel & Restaurant, 7 North Street,Onancock. Call 757-787-7400. In a building that was an early 1900s hotel, the Charlotte is a boutique hotel and gourmet restaurant that features a full-service bar, intimate dining room, and art gallery. Web site: http://www.thecharlotte hotel.com.

Inn at Onancock, 30 North Street, Onancock. Call 757-789-7711. Gourmet bed-and-breakfast within three blocks of the town wharf. Web site: http://www.innatonancock.com.

Rittenhouse Motor Lodge, 23054 Lankford Highway, Cape Charles. Call 757-331-27668. Old-style motor court in a park-like setting. Web site: http://www.rittenhousemotorlodge.com/.

Waterside Inn, Chincoteague Island, 3761 S. Main Street, Chincoteague Island. Call 877-870-3434. Waterfront rooms with private balconies. Web site: http://www.watersidemotorinn.com.

Attractions and Recreation

Barrier Islands Center, 7295 Young Street, Machipongo. Call 757-678-5550. At historic Almshouse Farm, the center celebrates the way of life of people who lived on Virginia's barrier islands. Web site: http://www.barrierislandscenter.com.

Broadwater Bay Eco-Tours, 6035 Killmon Point Road, Exmore. Call 757-442-4363. Guided tours of the Shore's barrier islands. Web site: http://www.broadwaterbayecotour.com.

Chatham Vineyards, 9232 Chatham Road, Machipongo. Call 757-678-5588. Winery is open to the public. Tours and tasting. Web site: http://www.chathamvineyards.net.

Chesapeake Bay Bridge-Tunnel. Call 757-331-2960. Spans 17 miles across the mouth of the Chesapeake Bay. One-way toll: $12. Enjoy a narrated drive, north- or south-bound, by downloading MP3 files from the web site: http://www.cbbt.com.

Chincoteague National Wildlife Refuge, 8231 Beach Road, Chincoteague. Call 757-336-3696. Highlights include Assateague Lighthouse, Assateague Island National Seashore, Herbert H. Bateman Educational and Administrative Center. Web site: http://www.fws.gov/northeast/chinco.

Eastern Shore of Virginia National Wildlife Refuge, 5003 Hallet Circle, Cape Charles. Call 757-331-2760. Visitor center, wildlife observation decks, walking trails. Web site: http://www.fws.gov/northeast/easternshore.

Eastern Shore Railway Museum, Parksley. Call 757-665-7245. Historic rail cars open to the public. Web site: http://www.parksley.com.

Kiptopeke State Park, 3540 Kiptopeke Drive, Cape Charles. Call 757-331-2267. Birding, boating, fishing, swimming, hiking, camping. Web site: http://www.dcr.virginia.gov/state_parks.

NASA Wallops Flight Facility Visitor Center, Wallops Island. Call 757-824-2298. Rockets, exhibits. Web site: http://www.wff.nasa.gov/vc.

SouthEast Expeditions, 32218 Lankford Highway, Cape Charles. Call 757-331-2680. Kayak tours and rentals. Web site: http://www.southeast expeditions.net.

Dining

AQUA Restaurant, 5 Marina Village Circle, Cape Charles. Call 757-331-8660. Seafood, seafood, seafood. Chesapeake Bay bouillabaisse anyone? Web site: http://www.baycreekresort.com.

Bay Creek Railway, 202 Mason Avenue, Cape Charles. Call 757-331-8770. Dining excursion train in a restored trolley. Web site: http://www.baycreekrailway.com.

Bill's Seafood Restaurant, 4040 Main Street, Chincoteague Island. Call 757-336-5831. Fresh seafood, hand-cut steaks, chops, pasta. Web site: http://www.billsseafoodrestaurant.com.

Bizzotto's Gallery & Caffé, 41 Market Street, Onancock. Call 757-787-3103. Gallery and restaurant, featuring international cuisine and local favorites such as crab cakes. Web site: http://bizzottos.esva.net.

Eastville Inn Restaurant, 16422 Courthouse Road, Eastville. Call 757-678-5745. Local seafood specialties in a casual fine-dining atmosphere. Web site: http://www.eastvilleinn.com.

J. H. West Seafood, 4150 Townsend Drive, Cape Charles. Call 757-331-3545. Unpretentious dining room inside a retail seafood shop. Excellent seafood. Web site: http://www.westseafood.net.

Kelly's Gingernut Pub, 133 Mason Avenue, Cape Charles. Call 757-331-3222. Watering hole and fine restaurant in an old bank building.

Mallards At The Wharf, 2 Market Street, Onancock. Call 757-787-8558. Wide-ranging menu that changes seasonally. Great atmosphere on the water. Web site: http://www.mallardsllc.com.

Sting-Ray's Restaurant, 26507 Lankford Highway, Cape Charles. Call 757-331-2505. Popular, sit-down seafood restaurant in the back of a gas station. Web site: http://www.cape-center.com.

Woody's Beach BBQ, 6700 Maddox Boulevard, Chincoteague. Call 757-336-5531. Outstanding barbecue and fried chicken sold at walk-up stands. Picnic tables available. Web site: http://www.woodysbeachbbq.com.

Wright's Seafood Restaurant, P.O. Box 130, Atlantic. Call 757-824-4012. Overlooking Watts Bay, near Chincoteague. Web site: http://www.wrightsrestaurant.com.

Other Contacts

Eastern Shore of Virginia Tourism. Call 757-787-8268. Web site: http://www.esvatourism.org.

Tangier is a wisp of an island in the middle of the Chesapeake Bay.

CHAPTER

2

Island Getaway

In the middle of the Chesapeake Bay, Tangier is a boat ride and a world away

Estimated length: 18 miles (by water) from Reedville
Estimated time: 2 days

Getting there: The easiest way is by passenger ferry. Seasonal ferries operate daily from Reedville, at the eastern end of US 360 on the mainland (or "western shore," as islanders refer to it) and from Onancock, just off US 13, on the Eastern Shore. A year-round ferry and mail boat that carries passengers operates between Tangier and Crisfield, Maryland. The island also has an airstrip for private planes and helicopters.

Highlights: The ferry ride across the **Chesapeake Bay**, strolling or riding a bicycle or golf cart along the island's narrow lanes (you will see only an occasional small car or pickup truck), the **Tangier History Museum and Interpretive Cultural Center**, the crab cakes, soft-shell crabs and other seafood, hearing the islanders' distinctive English dialect, and, in general, an up close view of life on **Tangier**.

It's late morning and as Captain Linwood Bowis deftly nestles the Chesapeake Breeze alongside the dock at Tangier Island, he reminds ferry passengers about to disembark of the day's schedule.

"Departure time this afternoon is 2:15," he says over the boat's public-address system. "If you miss it, no problem. I'll be back tomorrow."

The line always gets a laugh, but it's no joke. Unless you own or charter a boat or aircraft, a passenger ferry is your only way on or off the island. For those of us planning to stay the night, the pressure is off, and we can focus on finding the island's best crab cake or some other seafood delight for lunch. Everyone else checks their watches.

I stop at the Waterfront Restaurant, just a few steps from where I leave the Chesapeake Breeze. It's not so much a restaurant as a kitchen with a window for ordering, and a couple of open-sided shelters with picnic tables at the edge of the dock. The menu includes burgers, chicken, and a variety of sandwiches, but I didn't ride 90 minutes on a boat across the bay to eat a burger. I order a soft-shell crab sandwich—a Tangier specialty—that comes with a side of cole slaw and a bottle of iced tea. Total cost: $10. The lightly battered and fried crab arrives between two slices of white bread. It is very basic. It also is very good. I sit at a picnic table savoring it as gulls call and a breeze drifts across the small harbor. It's an excellent start to my visit.

After lunch, it's time to think about getting around the island. You can rent a golf cart or a bike, or, if you like guided tours you can catch a ride in one of several stretch golf carts waiting near the dock and be chauffeured around the island by a resident offering an expert description of the place.

This is my third trip to **Tangier**. I've come to know my way around the place, although considering the size of the shrinking island—a mile wide, 3 miles long, and mostly marshland—that's hardly a claim to fame. I've also come to develop an appreciation for the islanders, their heritage, and their warm hospitality.

Theirs is not an easy life. Erosion is taking their land, at a rate of about 9 acres a year, and modern realities are doing the same to their livelihoods. For generations, the men of Tangier made their livings crabbing in the waters around the island. But reduced crab populations and government regulations have forced watermen to find work elsewhere, as only a few dozen still crab for a living. Many leave the island, at least temporarily, to work on tugboats. Young islanders, seeking a more secure future, increasingly move to the mainland for other kinds of jobs and come back only to visit. The result: Tangier's population is down to just more than 500, far from its peak of 1,200 in the 1930s.

So, what you see as you walk around Tangier is not only a quaint little island, as it's often described by visitors, but, if circumstances don't change, a vanishing one.

The Tangier History Museum serves as a repository of the island's history and a visitor center for tourists.

Unhindered by time and knowing where I'm going, I choose to walk.

I stop first at the Tangier History Museum and Interpretive Cultural Center, a converted gift shop that tells the island's story in a charmingly down-home way. It also provides Tangier's only public restrooms, aside from those in the handful of restaurants on the island.

Locals and visitors gather on the inviting front porch for chitchat or games of checkers with colored seashells as game pieces. Inside the museum, photographs, newspaper and magazine clippings, and an extensive timeline tells the history of the island that for centuries, the story goes, was a hunting ground for Native Americans. The English didn't show up until 1608, when Captain John Smith came upon the island while exploring the bay.

Many of the descendants of English settlers who live on Tangier today speak with a thick Cornish accent. High tide is *hoi toid.*

You also can keep track of the last-name sweepstakes. About half of island residents have one of three last names: Parks, Pruitt, or Crockett. When I check the most recent count, I see the Parks family, numbering more than 100, has taken the lead. The Pruitts and Crocketts, both with more than 70 representatives, are jockeying for second place.

Besides name games, you can touch a crabpot and other tools of the watermen's trade, or watch a video featuring interviews with residents. Better yet, talk to an actual resident.

"Most of us are friendly and nice and love to see new faces on the island," said Gayle Laird, a native of Tangier and a regular volunteer at the museum. "I love it here. I wouldn't ever want to leave."

Two of the new faces stayed. Neil and Susan Kaye, physicians from Delaware, fell in love with the island on a visit, bought a weekend home, and have become driving forces in the community. They've helped develop various projects, including the museum, which has become a gathering spot for the community as much as a visitor center. They also set up the island's only public library, largely a collection of used books, in a shed across from their home, which they've dubbed Muddy Toes.

It's said once you get the marsh mud of Tangier between your toes, you'll always return.

"We think this is certainly a special place," said Neil Kaye, a psychiatrist. "The community's been wonderful."

Part of Tangier's appeal to the Kayes is what it is not. It is not a resort, and it is not Disney World. It is real. A little rough around the edges in spots, but very real. They want others to appreciate the island, as they do, for what it is.

"It is incredibly beautiful here," Kaye says. "You just have to open your eyes to see it."

For a different view of the island, I walk down a long boardwalk behind the museum to a floating dock where several kayaks are available for visitors to use at no charge. "Free kayaks," a visitor on the dock says to me, still not quite believing his good fortune, even though he's just finished a paddling tour. "Must be the only place on the planet where you can find this. It's a great idea."

It is indeed.

I climb in a green kayak and begin paddling the so-called Orange Trail, one of a series of designated water trails around and through the island. The Orange Trail follows a channel cut through the island's seagrass marsh, under four bridges (some of which have such low clearance during high tide that you will need to portage your kayak to the other side), and finally through the harbor, past crab boats and crab shanties, where crabs are sorted as they shed their shells and become soft crabs.

It takes about an hour to paddle around the island, but take your time. No rush.

A few random notes about Tangier:

- There are about 30 rooms for rent on the island, spread among three bed-and-breakfast inns: **Hilda Crockett's Chesapeake House**, the **Bay View Inn,** and the **Sunset Inn**. Reservations are highly recommended.

- There are five restaurants plus **Spanky's Place**, an ice cream shop with 1950s music. The **Double Six Sandwich Shoppe**, a hole-in-the-wall, early-morning hangout for watermen before they head out to work, also serves sandwiches and coffee, but it maintains only pre-dawn hours and most tourists aren't looking for food at 3 AM.

- The island has a single market, **Daley & Son Grocery**, a typical small-town store that sells a little bit of everything, and really jumps on Thursdays when the weekly supply boat arrives and the shelves are restocked. For serious shopping, islanders take the year-round ferry to **Crisfield**, where some keep cars, and then drive to **Salisbury**, the closest thing to a big city, which is one of the reasons many Tangier-men, as they're traditionally known, identify more with Maryland than Virginia.

- Looking for local art? Start at the museum, where paintings by artist-in-residence, Ken Castelli, are for sale. You might also meet Castelli, who helped design the museum and is often there chatting up visitors. For other local trinkets and publications, or the requisite T-shirt or cap, try one of several gift shops that are more than happy to have you drop by.

- Bring cash or credit cards because there are no banks or ATMS on the island.

- Cell phone service is unreliable.

- You won't find alcohol for sale on the island, but no one objects if you bring it with you and enjoy it discreetly and responsibly.

Back on dry land, I resume my stroll on the streets that are surprisingly busy, but not in the way most of us have come to think of busy streets. A young mother pushes her small child in a stroller. A father pedals a bicycle, his little girl in the basket. Golf carts putter past. A cat ambles beside me for a short distance before ducking through a gate. Cats are everywhere on Tangier, reportedly numbering in the hundreds. You can't travel far without seeing one sprawled lazily on a sidewalk or stealthily pursuing a seafood dinner.

I stop and read trail markers, some tacked to telephone poles, which offer nuggets about the island: the story behind certain homes, the account of long-gone wharves, the descriptions of wading birds such as great blue herons and snowy egrets that high-step gingerly through the marshes.

Tangiermen live in three distinct sections on the island, separated by marshes and connected by bridges. Their homes seem crowded together because they are: of the island's 700 acres, all but 80 are marshland, and even those 80 go under water when exceptionally high tides periodically wash over the island. With land at a premium, it's not unusual to find family cemeteries in front yards or wedged between homes.

Like any small town, Tangier's hodgepodge of houses includes a few structures that are rundown and boarded up. Others, though, are as pretty as pictures, surrounded by neatly trimmed yards and white picket fences, precisely what you would expect to find in an island paradise.

Swain Memorial United Methodist, constructed in the 1890s, is the island's centerpiece, a handsome white frame church whose steeple, along with the island's water tower, defines the Tangier skyline. The island's other church, New Testament Church, a non-denominational congregation that splintered from Swain in the 1940s, is just down the lane.

Faith and religion play vital roles in the island's history. When British troops occupied Tangier during the War of 1812, it was, as the story goes, a Methodist preacher, Joshua Thomas, the "parson of the islands," who was asked to deliver a sermon to the troops before their attack on Baltimore. Thomas preached that the British would be defeated, as they were. More recently, in the 1990s, island leaders turned down a Hollywood offer to have scenes of a Paul Newman-Kevin Costner movie, *Message in a Bottle,* filmed here because the script contained sex and swearing.

The island's schoolhouse sits behind Swain. Tangier Combined School, one of the last such schools in Virginia, houses K–12 under one roof. Enrollment is typically less than 100. They don't have many snow days here, but on occasion the school opens late or lets out early when high tides threaten to lap at the front steps.

It takes me a couple of hours to cover the island by foot, stopping along the way to enjoy the view and speak to passersby or those sitting, only a few

A dwindling number of Tangiermen make their livings working the waters of the Chesapeake Bay

feet away, on their front porches. By bicycle, you can ride everywhere in less than an hour.

For a truly different glimpse of the island, take a tour with a waterman such as Denny Crockett, who will show tourists where he pulls crab pots, and point out ospreys, eagles, and other wildlife along the way. I've gone with Denny on a tour—he's former principal of the island's school and also runs Hilda Crockett's Chesapeake House bed-and-breakfast and restaurant.

I've stayed at the Chesapeake House, which is actually two houses, across the lane from one another. Accommodations are as comfortable as the food is comforting. Meals are served family style, meaning guests sit together at tables, whether you know one another or not, and the lunch and dinner menus never vary: the bowls and platters of crab cakes, clam fritters, baked ham, corn pudding, potato salad, cole slaw, pickled beets, and homemade rolls keep coming until you've had your fill. Be sure to leave room for pound cake.

Dinner on this night, though, is at Fisherman's Corner Restaurant, which is operated by the wives of watermen. The menu includes an assortment of seafood dishes featuring crabs, clams, shrimp, and flounder. I can't get past the crab cakes, which are plump and as tasty as any I've had. A friend orders the filet of flounder "overstuffed" with crabmeat, which fills his plate.

For dessert, try an ice cream cone at Spanky's Place, or indulge in something with fewer calories: a sunset viewed from Tangier's wisp of a beach that curls around the southern end of the island. On this late summer evening, the pinks and oranges of the setting sun fill the sky, offering not only beauty but novelty: There are few places in Virginia where you can watch the sun sink into the sea.

The next day, I take a bike ride around the island, pedaling:

- Past the airstrip that was recently repaved

The narrow lanes of the island are perfect for strolling or touring the island by bicycle.

- Past the site of the new medical center (a mainland doctor helicopters in once a week to care for islanders, and a dentist does the same, although a physician's assistant and nurses live on the island)

- Past the dock, where retired watermen sit on benches and solve the world's problems, and the daily arrival of the mail boat from Crisfield is a happily anticipated event

- Past the volunteer fire department, a critical component on an island of wooden homes, which features a full-size fire truck and ambulance, and weekly fire alarm tests at noon on Saturdays

- Over a bridge to the small section known as Canton, where you find New Creations Salon, in the back of a home, for all of your hair, nails, and tanning needs

- Past the occasional soft-drink vending machine, stationed randomly alongside the roadway.

It's a kick to ride on 4-foot-wide strips of asphalt with official state route numbers and to see golf carts halt at the occasional stop sign. Watch your lead foot: The posted speed limit is 15 mph.

For my last lunch before departing, I stop at Lorraine's, a small sandwich shop tucked behind the grocery store.

"I wish I was on the road," says owner Lorraine Marshall, who's run the place since the mid-1980s. Location is as important on Tangier as anywhere else, since tourists pass at least three other restaurants before getting to her shop. But locals know where she is; hers is the only restaurant open year-round.

I order the day's special: a crab cake sandwich on a bun with cole slaw. Marshall's daughter, Jamie Bradshaw, who's helped her mom at the restaurant since she was a teenager, fries the crab cake while I take a seat at a back table.

The sandwich is, as I anticipate, terrific, and I polish it off quickly.

"Hope you enjoyed it!" Jamie says as I stand to go." Come back again."

I head to the dock where the tourists returning to Reedville wait patiently to board the Chesapeake Breeze, which, as Linwood Bowis promised, returned. Departure time, as we well know, is 2:15 PM.

Bowis, the second-generation boat captain and husband of a Tangier native, says not everyone who makes the trip to Tangier knows exactly what to expect. But in general, he says, ferry-goers enjoy traveling there on a boat and "seem to enjoy seeing something different."

The island's history attracts some visitors; the out-of-the-way nature of the place appeals to others.

"But some," Bowis said with a smile, "just want to eat a crab cake."

IN THE AREA

Accommodations

Bay View Inn Bed and Breakfast, 6408 W. Ridge Road. Call 757-891-2396. Web site: http://www.tangierisland.net. One of the oldest homes on the island. A country-style breakfast is served every morning. Open year-round.

Hilda Crockett's Chesapeake House, 16243 Main Ridge Road. Call 757-891-2331. Web site: http://www.chesapeakehousetangier.com. Hilda Crockett began providing lodging and home-cooked meals in 1939. Overnight stays include family-style breakfasts and lunch or dinner. Last seating is 5 PM. Open mid-April to mid-October.

Sunset Inn Bed and Breakfast, 16650 W. Ridge Road. Call 757-891-2535. Web site: http://www.tangierislandsunset.com. Motel-like accommodations include continental breakfast. Closed January, February, March.

Attractions

Tangier Island Museum and Interpretative Cultural Center, 16215 Main Ridge Road. Web site: http://www.tangierhistorymuseum.org.

Dining

Channel Marker Restaurant, 4409 Chambers Lane. Call 757-891-2220. Lunch and dinner. Fresh seafood.

Fisherman's Corner Restaurant, 4419 Long Bridge Road. Call 757-891-2900. Web site: http://www.fishermanscornerrestaurant.com. Lunch and dinner. Fresh seafood. From crab bisque to crab cakes. Average price: $10–20 per person.

Hilda Crockett's Chesapeake House, 16243 Main Ridge Road. Call 757-891-2331. Web site: http://www.chesapeakehousetangier.com. Breakfast, lunch, and dinner (last seating 5 PM), served family style. Breakfast, $9 per adult; lunch or dinner, $22 per adult.

Lorraine's Snack Bar, 4417 Chambers Lane. Call 757-891-2225. Lunch or dinner. Subs, sandwiches, pizza, milk shakes, and seafood. Eat in, take out, or delivery to local B&Bs. Open year-round.

Spanky's Place, 16200 Main Ridge Road. Call 757-891-2514. Ice cream, snacks, and 1950s music.

Waterfront Restaurant, on the dock. Call 757-891-2248. Lunch or late afternoon snack. Subs, sandwiches. Crab cakes and soft crabs. Delivery for overnight guests.

TRANSPORTATION

Ferries

From Reedville: Tangier-Rappahannock Cruises, 468 Buzzard Point Road, Reedville. Call 804-453-2628. Web site: http://www.tangiercruise .com. Daily cruises to Tangier, May through October. Round-trip $25 adults, $13 children.

From Onancock: Tangier-Onancock Ferry. Call 757-891-2505. Web site: http://www.tangierferry.com. Daily cruises to Tangier, May through October. Round-trip $25 adults, $5 children 5 and under.

From Crisfield, Maryland: Tangier Island Cruises, 1001 W. Main Street, Crisfield. Call 410-968-2338. Web site: http://www.tangierisland cruises.com. Daily cruises to Tangier, May through October. Round-trip $25 for adults ($35 for overnight stay), $12 children, ages 7–12 (children 6 and under free).

M& S Charters, Tangier. Call 757 891 2440. Web site: http://www .tangierisland-va.com/tangiercharters. Daily cruises to Tangier, year-round.

On Tangier: Bicycles and golf carts may be rented. For bicycles, contact **Waterfront Restaurant,** 757-891-2248. For golf carts, contact **Sunset Inn Bed & Breakfast,** 757-891-2535.

Other Contacts

Tangier Island Guide. For tours and other information about Tangier, visit http://www.tangierisland-va.com.

Wicomico Parish Church is one of many historic churches on the Northern Neck.

CHAPTER

3

The Northern Neck

Relax and leave your neckties at home

Estimated length: 100 miles
Estimated time: Weekend

Getting there: From Richmond, go east on US 360 to cross the Rappahannock River at Tappahannock, or, alternatively, follow VA 33 east through West Point and Saluda to cross the Rappahannock at White Stone, on the eastern end of the Northern Neck. From Washington and points north, use I-95 or US 301 to reach VA 3 or US 17, either of which will lead you to the Northern Neck.

Highlights: Leave the worries of the world behind with a drive through farms, forests, and small towns such as **Warsaw**, **Montross**, **Reedville**, **Kilmarnock,** and **Irvington**. Dip your toes or a fishing line in the Rappahannock or Potomac rivers or the **Chesapeake Bay**. Look for bald eagles or osprey at **Belle Isle State Park** or colonial architecture at **Historic Christ Church**. Enjoy a meal at one of the Northern Neck's fine restaurants, be it on the waterfront or in a converted gas station.

The true, laid-back spirit of the Northern Neck is amply displayed all over this watery retreat, but nowhere more affectionately than in a cemetery behind Wicomico Parish Church in the village of Wicomico Church. There, on the gravestone of John Carr Clarke Byrne, a longtime Neck resident who died at age 80 in 1995, are these words: I'D RATHER BE ON MILL CREEK.

Mill Creek is only one of many preferred destinations on the Northern Neck, or simply, The Neck, as locals know it, a lush peninsula bounded by the Potomac River to the north, the Rappahannock River to the south, and the Chesapeake Bay to the east. George Washington, who was born here, called this place "the garden of Virginia." As for its name, "Neck," according to the Northern Neck Tourism Council, comes from the Old English word for "a narrow piece of land with water on each side." "Northern" comes from the fact it is Virginia's northernmost peninsula along the bay.

Since bridges replaced ferries in the 20th century and made this area more accessible to outlying areas, The Neck has become a popular weekend and summer getaway for city folk, who covet its easygoing pace. Indeed, those who come here regularly to unwind report their blood pressure drops and a weight lifts from their shoulders as soon as they see I-95 fading in their rear-view mirror or they cross a bridge onto The Neck. Your biggest worry here should be where to find a good crab cake.

Arranging to meet a friend on a weekday at his office in Kilmarnock, one of The Neck's more picturesque little towns, I do not want to appear underdressed so I ask if I should wear a tie. "No neckties," he says, "on The Neck."

Though a popular destination, The Neck hasn't changed much in appearance over the years. It has avoided the explosive growth that often plagues rural areas revealed as little slices of paradise. The Neck remains largely farms and forests, interrupted by small towns such as Warsaw, Montross, and Reedville. Homes of all types—from massive mansions to tiny weekend cottages—pepper the shoreline. About 20 percent of its population is age 65 and over, more than a third higher than the rate in the rest of Virginia.

Naturally, water is the area's greatest distinction. With more than 1,100 miles of shoreline counting the bay, rivers, creeks, and inlets, The Neck has been home to generations of watermen, recreational sailors and anglers, and explorers. Captain John Smith left Jamestown to sail the Potomac and Rappahannock rivers in the early 1600s. Today, bird-watchers do most of the discovering on The Neck, with eagles and ospreys among the residents, but there are plenty of other prizes—history, nature, and wineries—to find, too. Not many traffic lights, either.

With a variety of entry points onto The Neck, you can make a driving tour of the area going in almost any direction. Be assured, you can turn off any little side road and find something worthy of exploration. You likely won't get lost; you'll run into water eventually. For general touring, you probably will want to use some combination of US 360 and VA 3, the primary roads in the region.

We typically begin our tours of The Neck crossing the bridge over the Rappahannock from Tappahannock on US 360. A note about Tappahannock: If hunger strikes before crossing the river, try Lowery's Seafood Restaurant, a family operation since 1938 that specializes in local oysters and crab.

Once across the river, it's decision time: Warsaw, 6 miles beyond the bridge, marks the intersection of US 360 and VA 3. Warsaw, by the way, is indeed named for the city in Poland. The town was called Richmond County Courthouse until 1830, when residents renamed it Warsaw in sympathy with the Polish struggle for independence. If you take VA 3 to the north, you go to Montross. If you take VA 3 south, it heads toward Kilmarnock. If you continue to head east on US 360, Reedville is the ultimate destination, as the road dead-ends just before splashing into Cockrell Creek.

Here's a sample of what you'll find, no matter which way you go:

Drive north on VA 3, and you will come upon Montross in 12 miles. On the way, stop at Hutt's, a popular produce stand near Lyells, where you'd be well advised to pick up a couple of quarts of local strawberries in late spring, or other fresh, just-picked fruits and vegetables at other times of the year. In Montross, grab a bite at casual spots such as Angelo's, Yesterday's, or The Art of Coffee, or maybe even a six-pack of the local favorite: Northern Neck Ginger Ale. Stop and shop at Carrot Cottage, a colorful emporium of eclectic merchandise.

The seat of Westmoreland County, Montross boasts a courthouse that dates to 1707 and, on its grounds, the nation's first sculptured Vietnam War Memorial. If you've never seen a lock of George Washington's hair, step into the nearby Westmoreland County Museum and Visitor Center. Washington's birthplace is not 10 miles away, on the Potomac.

If you're in an exploring mood, venture over to VA 606, between Kinsale and Tucker Hill, and search out the oldest church in Westmoreland County, Yeocomico Church. The Neck, besides having a number of eateries occupying former filling stations, is full of churches. George Washington attended the church, first built in 1655 and rebuilt in 1706. Author John Dos Passos is buried in the cemetery.

To reach Reedville, start at Warsaw and go east on US 360 for just over 30 miles, through Callao and Heathsville, where you might want to stop at

Rice's Hotel/Hughlett's Tavern, a restored 1700s structure that now houses a blacksmith shop, restaurant, and gift shop. Then, it's on to Reedville, reputed to be the wealthiest community in the nation in the early 1900s because of the menhaden fishing industry. The industry is much reduced, but the stately Victorian mansions built by those early boat captains and factory owners remain along the last stretch of US 360. Millionaires Row, some of the locals call it.

The Reedville Fishermen's Museum tells the story of the area's watermen and their reliance on the bay and its tributaries for their livelihoods. A restored skipjack and a replica of the boat John Smith built to explore the bay more than 400 years ago are among the displays. If you're ready for lunch or dinner, two locally owned, family-friendly choices: Tommy's Restaurant, with local seafood and views overlooking the water, is a good bet, as is the Crazy Crab, at the very end of the road, with, naturally, numerous crab dishes and a waterfront deck.

If you're in the mood for something sweeter, say, ice cream, Chitterchats Ice Cream & Gossip Parlor awaits, with homemade ice cream in great waffle cones. I highly recommend a double scoop of cookie dough ice cream. The shop is directly across the street from The Gables Bed & Breakfast, a five-story brick mansion that was built by a wealthy boat captain and remains perhaps the most impressive house on The Neck.

Yeocomico Church, well off the well-traveled path, is the final resting place of author John Dos Passos.

Vineyards and wineries are sprouting around The Neck, and several are open for tastings and tours:

Athena Vineyards and Winery, 3138 Jesse Dupont Memorial Highway, Heathsville. Web site: http://www.athenavineyards.com.

Belle Mount Vineyards, 2570 Newland Road, Warsaw. Call 804-333-4700. Web site: http://www.bellemount.com.

The Hague Winery, 8268 Cople Highway, Hague. Call 804-472-5283. Web site: http://www.thehaguewinery.com.

Ingleside Vineyards, 5872 Leedstown Road, Oak Grove. Call 804-224-8687. Web site: http://www.inglesidevineyards.com.

Oak Crest Vineyard & Winery, 8215 Oak Crest Drive, King George. Call 540-663-2813. Web site: http://www.oakcrestwinery.com.

Vault Field Vineyards, 2953 Kings Mill Road, Kinsale. Call 804-472-4430. Web site: http://www.vaultfield.com.

White Fences Vineyard Winery, 170 White Fences Vineyard Winery, Irvington. (Look for the giant corkscrew sculptures.) Call 804-438-5559. Web site: http://www.whitefencesvineyard.com.

The daily ferry to Tangier Island, mid-May until mid-October, leaves from Buzzard's Point Marina, just across the creek from the town itself and accessible by way of Fairport Road, just east of Reedville off US 360. Likewise, the seasonal ferry to Smith Island, another bay island just north of Tangier (and in Maryland waters), departs daily from the northern side of Reedville. Take US 360 through Burgess, then turn left on Sunny Bank Road, follow it for 2 miles and then go right on Campground Road.

Driving on The Neck requires a little patience and a little planning, since everything seems to be about 20 minutes from everything else—like driving from Reedville to Kilmarnock. From Reedville head back west on US 360 to Burgess, then turn south on VA 200 (aka Jessie Ball Dupont Memorial Highway). Before you get to Kilmarnock, though, turn left on VA 606 (Shiloh School Road) to VA 605 (Balls Neck Road). Head left to the Dameron Marsh Natural Area Preserve or right to Hughlett Point Natural Area Preserve. Both state-protected wisps of land jut into the bay. At Dameron, flanked by Mill Creek, walk in solitude on a gravel road through the marsh, a haven for birds and other critters. It's lovely, but take along bug spray.

Back to VA 200, continue to Kilmarnock, a tidy little town, excellent for

Reedville marks the eastern end of the road for US 360.

walking, with numerous interesting shops, such as Kilmarnock Antique Gallery and Rappahannock Art League Studio. When you need a bite to eat, try any number of casual, reasonably priced dining spots: Town Bistro, Dixie Deli, Lee's Restaurant, Car Wash Café (where you can actually get a car wash and fill your vehicle with gas), or even Rappahannock General Hospital, whose cafeteria is decent, open to the public and, because breakfast or lunch can be had for less than $4, known in some quarters as "the best deal in town." Or you can stop at one of my favorites: Savannah Joe's Bar-B-Que, an unpretentious, order-at-the-counter sort of place in a former gas station in a supermarket parking lot. The pulled pork combo—cole slaw and all—is outstanding.

From Kilmarnock, go south on either VA 3 to White Stone or VA 200 to Irvington. Both roads eventually meet anyway. White Stone, like every other town on The Neck, offers good food possibilities: Willaby's, a coffee shop and café serving breakfast and lunch, and Rocket Billy's, a trailer-turned-food-stand with as good a fried soft-shell crab sandwich as you can find.

Irvington is a great little community, best known, perhaps, for Christ Church, a restored Colonial-era church built by Robert "King" Carter, a powerful and wealthy landowner at the turn of the 18th century, and Tides Inn, a renowned resort (with golf course). But Irvington also offers the Steamboat Era Museum—which, as you might expect, celebrates the steamboat era of the region, the 1800s and early 1900s—eclectic shops, and

The Hope & Glory Inn, a romantic bed-and-breakfast in a 19th-century, butter yellow schoolhouse. One of its amenities: an outdoor shower with claw-footed tub so you can bathe, privately, but under the stars. Food? Look no further than Nate's Trick Dog Café, a small place that gets big reviews.

To complete a driving loop of The Neck, head north on VA 3, back toward Warsaw, but for a change of pace turn off on VA 201 at Lively, go 3 miles, then right on VA 354 for another 3 miles, and then left on VA 683 to the entrance to Belle Isle State Park, one of the Virginia's newest. Trails for hiking, biking, and horseback riding follow old farm roads through fields and marshes. Bikes and canoes are available for rent. Walking might be best, though, for stopping and watching in quiet awe through binoculars at, say, a trio of bald eagles, perched in a treetop a few hundred yards in the distance. Ospreys are everywhere. Same for great blue herons. The place is a wonderland for bird-watchers.

It's like my friend, Jann Steele, a long-time, part-time resident of The Neck, tells me when we stop on an empty road to admire a picture-perfect view of a gently moving creek.

"One of the things I love about the Northern Neck," says Steele, who lives in the tiny community of Sharps, a former steamship town, "is you can go around a curve and feel like you're in the middle of a wilderness where no one has ever been."

IN THE AREA

Accommodations

The Gables, 859 Main Street, Reedville. Call 804-453-5209. Victorian mansion bed-and-breakfast on town's historic Main Street. Web site: http://www.thegables.com.

Holiday Inn Express, 599 N. Main Street, Kilmarnock. Call 804-436-1500. Web site: http://www.ichotelsgroup.com/h/d/ex/1/en/home.

The Hope and Glory Inn, 65 Tavern Road, Irvington. Call 800-497-8228. Old schoolhouse converted into a bed-and-breakfast inn. Web site: http://www.hopeandglory.com.

The Tides Inn, 480 King Carter Drive, Irvington. Call 804-438-5000. Luxury resort on its own peninsula. Web site: http://www.tidesinn.com.

Part-time Neck residents Jann and Mike Steele keep their eyes on a family of bald eagles at Belle Isle State Park.

Attractions and Recreation

Rice's Hotel/Hughlett's Tavern, 73 Monument Place, Heathsville. Call 804-580-3377. Restored 1700s building with blacksmith forge, quilt guild, tavern restaurant, and gift shop. Web site: http://www.rhhtfoundation.org.

Belle Isle State Park, 1632 Belle Isle Road, Lancaster. Hiking trails, canoeing, birding. Call 804-462-5030. Web site: http://www.dcr.virginia.gov/state_parks/bel.shtml.

Historic Christ Church, P.O. Box 24, Irvington. Call 804-438-6855. Completed in 1735, Christ Church is a well-preserved example of Colonial Virginia's parish churches. Open for tours. Web site: http://www.christchurch1735.org.

Reedville Fishermen's Museum, 504 Main Street, Reedville. Call 804-453-6529. Preserves heritage of maritime history of lower Chesapeake Bay. Web site: http://www.rfmuseum.org.

Dining

Good Eats Café, 12720 Cople Highway, Kinsale. Call 804-472-4385. Gourmet dining in a renovated 1930s gas station. Web site: http://www.goodeatscafe.net.

Lancaster Tavern, 8373 Mary Ball Road, Lancaster. Call 804-462-0080. Northern Neck tradition of fine dining. Also a bed-and-breakfast. Web site: http://lancastertavern.com.

Lowery's Seafood Restaurant, 528 S. Church Lane, Tappahannock. Call 804-443-2800. Favorite family dining spot since the 1930s. Web site: http://www.lowerysrestaurant.com.

Nate's Trick Dog Café, 4357 Irvington Road, Irvington. Call 804-438-6363. Fine dining in a small place that gets rave reviews from locals and visitors. Web site: http://www.trickdogcafe.com.

Northern Neck Gourmet, 115 Main Street, Warsaw. Call 804-333-3012. Lunch café, deli, wines, and cheeses, as well as weekly tapas specials. Web site: http://www.northernneckgourmet.com.

Savannah Joe's Bar-B-Que, 55 Irvington Road, Kilmarnock. Pit-cooked barbecued pork, ribs, chicken. Web site: http://www.smokinjoesbarbeque.com.

The Oaks, 5434 Mary Ball Road, Lively. Call 804-462-7050. Down-home place with monster crab cakes.

Town Bistro, 62 Irvington Road, Kilmarnock. Call 804-435-0070. Casual upscale dining in an intimate setting. Web site: http://www.townbistro.com.

Other Contacts

Northern Neck Tourism Council, P.O. Box 1707, Warsaw. Call 804-333-1919. Web site: http://www.Northernneck.org.

Visitors can board re-creations of the Susan Constant, Godspeed, *and* Discovery *at Jamestown Settlement.*   JAMESTOWN-YORKTOWN FOUNDATION

CHAPTER

4

Historic Triangle

A short drive, a long day, and 400 years of American history

Estimated length: 23 miles
Estimated time: Day trip

Getting there: To reach **Jamestown** from I-64, take Exit 242A and take VA 199 west to either the Colonial Parkway or VA 31, and follow the signs. Or for an altogether different approach, come from the south side of the **James River,** taking VA 10 to VA 31 north to the free **Jamestown-Scotland Ferry.** Coming across the water to Jamestown will afford you a modern-day view of what the first colonists saw upon arriving there.

Highlights: Visiting **Jamestown, Colonial Williamsburg,** and **Yorktown,** historic sites that represent, one could argue, the birthplace of the United States, all connected by the scenic, 23-mile **Colonial Parkway.** Jamestown is where America was born, Williamsburg is where its system of government was nurtured, and Yorktown is where the young nation won its independence.

You can't very well make a serious tour of Virginia without hitting a site or two of where it all started: the historic triangle of Jamestown, Williamsburg, and Yorktown. It can be an enlightening and moving experience.

Stand on the deck of the *Discovery,* the 66-foot-long, full-size replica of the tiny ship that sailed from London in 1606, and gaze out over the bow. Imagine the placid waters of the James River are heaving swells in the

53

Atlantic, and, if your imagination is vivid enough, you get some sense of what it must have been like for the colonists aboard, heading into the great unknown. Four months they were on that ship. Only slightly less amazing than the fact they reached the New World intact is that they didn't kill each other in the process. Their boat was small and cramped, their provisions limited, their patience thin.

Many of them, in fact, did not survive long-term in the place they named Jamestown, but the settlement did, and America was born.

The *Discovery,* along with replicas of its larger sister ships, *Susan Constant* and *Godspeed,* are usually moored and available for boarding at Jamestown Settlement, a sprawling indoor and outdoor museum that tells the story of America's first permanent English settlement through gallery exhibits, film, and living history. Hanging around Jamestown Settlement and the adjacent Historic Jamestowne, the original site of the colony that's now jointly administered by the National Park Service and Preservation Virginia, is at once an instructive and humbling experience. What must it have been like to try to build a life here, so far from all they knew and in the face of terrible hardships such as illness and famine, not to mention fear and loneliness?

Our plan is to start at Jamestown, then drive 10 miles east along the Colonial Parkway to Colonial Williamsburg, grab some lunch and see some sights, then drive another 13 miles to the eastern end of the parkway at Yorktown. It will be a full day.

First, a note about admission fees. Jamestown Settlement and Yorktown Victory Center are operated by the Jamestown-Yorktown Foundation, a state agency. Tickets may be purchased for each or in combination. In 2010, rates were $14 for adults to visit Jamestown Settlement and $9.50 for Yorktown Victory Center. A ticket for both could be had for $19.25. Children ages 6–12 were about half of those prices. Historic Jamestowne and Yorktown Battlefield carry National Park Service admission fees. Visitors can purchase a Colonial National Historical Park Pass that will gain them entry to both for seven days. At the time of our visit, the price was $10, with children 15 and under free.

At Jamestown Settlement, we come first to the theater and galleries, so we watch a film that provides context for what we're about to see outside, and we browse exhibits arranged in a helpful time line that cover the convergence of English, Native American, and African American cultures. We walk outdoors, through the huts of a re-created Powhatan Indian Village

The Governor's Palace is one of the most popular sites in Colonial Williamsburg.
COLONIAL WILLIAMSBURG FOUNDATION, WILLIAMSBURG, VA.

where historical interpreters are making rope. At other times, they grind corn, make tools, and perform any number of other routine daily tasks from 400 years ago. The walkway leads to James Fort, a re-creation of the triangular-shaped fort constructed by the colonists that includes wattle-and-daub houses with thatched roofs, a church, and a blacksmith shop, where a demonstration is taking place. Then, it's down to the dock, and a few minutes exploring the ships.

If all of this history leaves you hungry, Jamestown Settlement Café, back in the museum's main building just down the hall from the ticket counter, offers the requisite burgers and sandwiches, but also Brunswick stew, vegetarian chili, and even homemade bread pudding with apple-raisin sauce for dessert.

To reach Historic Jamestowne, about a mile away, get on the Colonial Parkway at Jamestown Settlement and head east along the river. The visitor center offers a short film and exhibits. We walk past the statue of Pocahontas where children are posing for family snapshots, and then past the nearby church tower, the only 17th-century building still standing at Jamestown. The church itself was built in 1906, on the site of several previous churches that either burned or fell into disrepair.

We continue down to the river, where we find the site of the original fort where Captain John Smith and the rest of the colonists lived. A guide tells me the fort wasn't as close to the water as it appears; in the early 1600s the shoreline was maybe the distance of a football field out into where the river is now. Erosion is the culprit. As we stand on the seawall, I notice the river lapping gently, but persistently, at the bank.

Those first colonists had a tough time, and it wasn't all their doing. Studies indicate they showed up in Jamestown during the worst drought in 800 years. We stroll along the shore and peek into an ongoing archaeological dig site. We see some of the discovered items at the Voorhees Archaearium, which masterfully uses scientific research and artifacts such as shards of pottery, surgical tools, and a human skeleton to tell the settlement's story.

Off to Colonial Williamsburg we head, but before we get away from Jamestown, we stop at the Jamestown glasshouse near the entrance to the park and watch artisans demonstrating the techniques of 17th-century glassblowing, which happened to be one of the first industries at Jamestown.

Colonial Williamsburg, the reconstructed colonial capital, is a 10-mile ride along the Colonial Parkway, the limited-access, three-lane road—the middle lane is for passing—with no commercial development to detract from its natural setting. The maximum speed limit is 45 miles per hour. The parkway, a unit of the National Park Service, traverses the peninsula from the James River to the York River, connecting the two NPS properties: Historic Jamestowne and Yorktown Battlefield. Colonial Williamsburg is in the middle.

Williamsburg thrived as Virginia's capital for most of the 1700s, before it was moved to Richmond. By the early 1900s, however, much of the historic town had fallen into disrepair. Philanthropist John D. Rockefeller Jr. spearheaded an effort to restore the town, and now it thrives as a major tourist attraction.

We arrive and park at the Colonial Williamsburg visitor center, just off the parkway and US 60. The parking lot is huge, and the center itself, where tickets are purchased and information gathered, has the feel of an airline terminal. On the same site, you'll find the Williamsburg Cascades Motel, Williamsburg Woodlands Hotel and Suites, and Huzzah! Restaurant. Shuttles are available to the historic area, but we opt to walk on a foot bridge that carries us first through Great Hopes Plantation, a living history site that's representative of rural Virginia in the 1700s, and then over and under roadways into the town itself.

There is much to do and see in Colonial Williamsburg, from demonstrations by shoemakers and chocolate makers to tours of the Governor's Palace and Bruton Parish Church. One thing to remember: You can visit Colonial Williamsburg and walk up and down the streets to your heart's content, but you must purchase an admission ticket to enter many of the buildings. There are various levels of tickets that provide various levels of access and tours, but the basic admission pass, in 2010, was $36 for adults and $18 for children ages 6 through 17.

We roam up and down Duke of Gloucester Street—the central avenue in the historic district—and stick our noses in the apothecary, the blacksmith's, and a tavern or two. We watch and listen as a fife-and-drum corps marches past. No cars here, just horse-drawn carriages. We walk around the

Living history performers portraying Gen. George Washington and the Marquis de Lafayette make an announcement about the siege of Yorktown and the final battle of the American Revolution.   COLONIAL WILLIAMSBURG FOUNDATION, WILLIAMSBURG, VA.

old capitol and over to the Governor's Palace, where we go around back to the formal gardens where we get lost, briefly, in the tall hedgerow maze. I remember this as a kid, coming here on school field trips, and I still think it's one of the neatest things in town.

We stop at the bakery behind the Raleigh Tavern and purchase ginger-bread and peanut butter cookies, apple cider and root beer, and enjoy them at a picnic table in the shade behind the shop. Now that we've had dessert, we head for lunch at the other end of Duke of Gloucester, at The Cheese Shop in Merchants Square (near an entrance to the College of William and Mary). The gourmet food shop, a favorite of locals and tourists, which often makes for long lines, sells all kinds of cheeses, naturally, but also great sandwiches. I go with the Virginia ham salad on rye, while my son settles on a small tub of freshly made mixed-bean salad. We are both pleased with our choices, as we enjoy lunch at tables on the front patio, a great vantage point for people-watching. Numerous shops and restaurants in the Merchants Square area make this an easy place to spend a considerable amount of time.

Yorktown, site of the climactic battle of the American Revolution, is another 13 miles east on the parkway, and, like Jamestown, it has two major attractions: Yorktown Victory Center and Yorktown Battlefield, both of which chronicle the colonial experience to the end of the war, which culminated in the surrender of British General Charles Lord Cornwallis at Yorktown in 1781.

Yorktown Victory Center, a sister park of Jamestown Settlement, offers a film and galleries as well as outdoor exhibits, such as a Continental army encampment that details the harsh realities of life as a soldier during the revolution, and a 1780s farm layout that demonstrates the way many Virginians lived in that era. Costumed historical interpreters lead hands-on activities.

Yorktown Battlefield, a unit of the National Park Service, offers a visitor center with artifacts such as General George Washington's military tents, and ranger-led programs or self-guided driving and walking tours of the battlefield. We walk on trails among the earthworks and cannon and admire the view of sailboats on the river. We cross a long pedestrian bridge over a ravine to reach the Yorktown Victory Monument. Nearly 100 feet tall, the monument to commemorate the victory over the British was authorized by the Continental Congress in October 1781. Construction began—a century later. The monument was finally completed in 1884.

Visitors can roam the Yorktown Battlefield on a bluff above the York River.

Yorktown, which sits on a bluff high above the river, looks like a colonial town with narrow streets and grand old houses, one of which belonged to Thomas Nelson Jr., who signed the Declaration of Independence. Daylight fading, we negotiate a narrow footpath down the hill to the waterfront where we find, beneath the bluff, Cornwallis' Cave, its small opening blocked by a gate and marked by a sign. As the story goes, Cornwallis moved his headquarters to the cave to escape the assault by American and French troops. More likely, the cave was used by a British gun crew to defend against the French fleet. As the story also goes, the cave is haunted, though we decide not to hang around to find out.

While the streets above are fairly quiet, the waterfront is far busier, even on a weeknight. We stroll past Yorktown Pub, its doors open to the warm evening and music spilling out. Just a few feet from the beach and something of a landmark, the popular pub attracts locals and tourists with fresh seafood, homemade desserts, and a convivial atmosphere. Farther down the bricked-over, waterfront path, we come to Riverwalk Landing, a multi-million-dollar retail development trying to capture a little waterfront magic with shopping and dining in this once thriving seaport. Nick's Riverwalk Restaurant is the big draw, and is actually two restaurants, one serving a casual fine-dining menu of seafood, beef, lamb, and poultry, and the other a café focusing on sandwiches, salads, and light fare. Nick's offers terrific views of the river, as well as the George P. Coleman Bridge, a 3,750-foot-long double-swing-span bridge over the river that connects Yorktown to Gloucester County. As we look up, we see the headlights of cars and trucks heading into the dusk. In less than 25 miles, we have traveled more than 400 years through American history. Not a bad day's work.

IN THE AREA

Accommodations

Great Wolf Lodge Resort, 549 East Rochambeau Drive, Williamsburg. Call 757-229-9700. Indoor water park, lodging, dining, and spa. Web site: http://www.greatwolf.com.

Colonial Williamsburg Resort, P.O. Box 1776, Williamsburg. Call 757-229-1000. Variety of lodging types, from motel to premium hotel. Web site: http://www.colonialwilliamsburgresort.com.

Attractions and Recreation

Busch Gardens, One Busch Gardens Boulevard, Williamsburg. Theme park. Seasonal. Call 1-800-343-7946. Web site: http://www.buschgardens.com.

Colonial National History Park, including **Historic Jamestowne, Yorktown Battlefield,** and **Colonial Parkway,** P.O. Box 210, Yorktown. Call 757-898-2410. Web site: http://www.nps.gov/colo.

Colonial Williamsburg, P.O. Box 1776, Williamsburg. Call 757-229-1000. Web site: http://www.history.org.

Jamestown Settlement and Yorktown Victory Center, P.O. Box 1607, Williamsburg. Call 757-253-4838. Web site: http://www.historyisfun.org.

Water Country USA, 176 Water Country Parkway, Williamsburg. Call 1-800-343-7946. Outdoor water park. Seasonal. Web site: http://www.watercountryusa.com.

Williamsburg Winery, 5800 Wessex Hundred, Williamsburg. Call 757-229-0999. Daily tours and tastings. Web site: http://www.williamsburg winery.com.

Dining

Nick's Riverwalk Restaurant, 323 Water Street, Suite A-1, Yorktown. Call 757-875-1522. Casual fine dining, as well as sandwiches and salads. Web site: http://www.riverwalkrestaurant.net.

Pierce's Pitt Bar-B-Que, 447 East Rochambeau, Williamsburg. Call 757-565-2955. Barbecue, burgers, hot dogs, and chicken. Web site: http://www.pierces.com.

The Cheese Shop, 410 W. Duke of Gloucester Street, Williamsburg. Call 757-220-0298. Sandwiches, cheese, freshly baked breads, specialty foods, wine cellar.

The Trellis, 403 Duke of Gloucester Street, Williamsburg. Call 757-229-8610. Fine dining. Web site: http://www.thetrellis.com.

Yorktown Pub, 112 Water Street, Yorktown. Pub fare and friendly, welcoming environment. Call 757-886-9964.

Other Contacts

Jamestown-Scotland Ferry, 16289 Rolfe Highway, Surry. Call 1-800-823-3779. Web site: http://www.vdot.virginia.gov/travel/ferry-james town.asp.

Greater Williamsburg Chamber and Tourism Alliance, 421 N. Boundary Street, Williamsburg. Call 757-229-6511. Web site: http://www .visitwilliamsburg.com.

Eleven generations of the Hill-Carter family have lived at Shirley Plantation.

CHAPTER

5

These Old Houses

The James River plantations radiate splendor and history

Estimated length: 40 miles
Estimated time: Day trip

Getting there: From downtown Richmond, take Main Street east to where it meets VA 5 and follow road to Jamestown. From the north side of Richmond, take Laburnum Avenue south to VA 5, or New Market Road, then head east. Or, by way of I-295, go to Exit 22A and then east on VA 5.

Highlights: A drive along VA 5, the old river road between Richmond and Jamestown. Tours of several of the grand **James River** plantations—**Berkeley**, **Shirley**, and **Sherwood Forest**—that represent the first westward expansion of English-speaking America and almost 400 years of the nation's history. For lunch or dinner, the **Charles City Tavern** is the spot.

How do you begin a history field trip? With doughnuts, of course. We stop at Country Style Donuts, regarded by many as having the best doughnuts in Richmond, and pick up a dozen of assorted varieties.

In an undistinguished building on the east side of town, meaning it's on our way to VA 5, Country Style serves up freshly made doughnuts 24 hours a day. You'll find regulars perched on stools at the counter at just about any hour, drinking their coffee and giving one another a hard time. The fritters, which are the size of small New England states, beckon me from the display case, but I am restrained and do not answer their call.

I stick with the doughnuts we've ordered, so we take our box of goodness, hop in the car, and head to the plantations—before I lose my will and change my mind about the fritters.

From the doughnut shop, we head east briefly on Williamsburg Road to Laburnum Avenue, turn right and drive not quite 5 miles to reach VA 5, also known as New Market Road before it becomes John Tyler Memorial Highway. We turn left and head east. My 12-year-old son and I each pluck a doughnut from the box.

History also is within easy reach. Shirley Plantation, the westernmost of the great Colonial plantations along the north bank of the James River and on our itinerary, is only 10 miles east of I-295. We barely have time to finish a doughnut before we turn right onto Shirley Plantation Road and drive for 2 miles past fields of corn and wheat to reach the house itself.

Shirley, like the other plantations we'll visit, is privately owned, but open to the public through regular visiting hours or by appointment. At Shirley, 11 generations of the Hill-Carter family have lived and worked here and still do. The 800-acre plantation, established in 1613, only 6 years after the colonists arrived at Jamestown, is considered the oldest family-owned business in North America. Tobacco was the early ticket to prosperity; the plantation has diversified since. The brick mansion was completed in 1738.

A guide rings a bell to signal the beginning of a tour of the great house. We learn the name Shirley comes from the British couple—the wife's maiden name was Shirley—who were given the royal land grant for the property in 1613. They never set foot on the land, but the name stuck. We admire the exquisite "flying staircase" that rises three stories without any visible means of support; the guide says hidden wrought-iron straps secure the stairs to the walls. We see a baby bed where Robert E. Lee slept; his mother, Anne Hill Carter, was born here, and she was married to Henry "Light Horse Harry" Lee in the parlor. Despite that connection, Union soldiers spared the home during the Civil War because of kindnesses shown by the family toward the troops. General George McClelland issued an order protecting the house from looting. The tour includes the downstairs only, because the 11th generation lives upstairs.

Outside, we stand on the lawn, in the shade of a massive 350-year-old willow oak, and look out over the James. We walk among the plantation's outbuildings and through the landscaped gardens, and then over to the corn crib where we meet plantation director Janet Appel, who half-jokingly also goes by The Chicken Whisperer, and we hold Kabob the Roos-

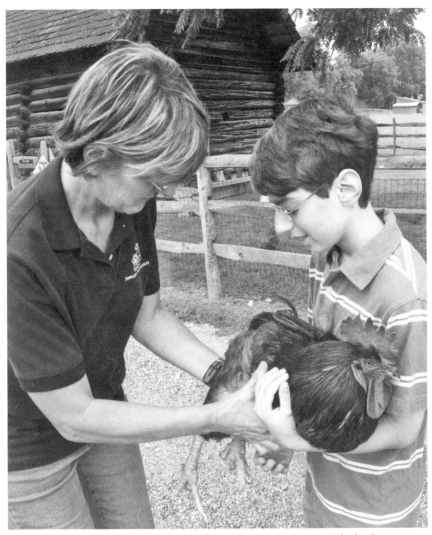

Shirley Plantation director Janet Appel introduces a visitor to Kabob, the rooster, a friendly bird who lives at Shirley, which is still a working plantation.

ter, a friendly and apparently good-humored bird that is a favorite among visiting school groups.

VA 5 is a pleasant, two-lane road that rambles along the north shore of the James. Historic markers, sometimes clumped together, are common sights along the roadside. Most have pull-off areas so you can safely stop and read. Otherwise, there isn't much to distract you among the forests and farmland: an occasional house, an intersecting road here and there, and the Virginia Capital Trail, a 50-mile-long pedestrian and bicycle trail along much of VA 5 that's being built in phases and will eventually connect Richmond, Jamestown, and Williamsburg.

We stop next at Berkeley, just 3 miles east of Shirley. A lot has happened here. The first official Thanksgiving in America—at least, to Virginians' way of thinking—was held here in 1619, beating the Pilgrims at Plimouth Plantation by 2 years. Benjamin Harrison V, a signer of the Declaration of Independence, and William Henry Harrison, ninth president of the United States, were born here. (The 23rd president, Benjamin Harrison, was a grandson of William Henry Harrison, but he was born and grew up in Ohio.) In 1862, McClelland set up his headquarters and supply base for 140,000 troops, one of whom composed "Taps" and played it for the first time. President Lincoln came here twice that summer to confer with McClelland and review the troops.

I have a few minutes before the next house tour begins, so I stroll

Berkeley Plantation was the site of America's first Thanksgiving.

through the terraced boxwood gardens, past the magnolia and crape myrtle trees, then walk down a long tree-sheltered lane to the river, gently lapping at the shore. I return to the house and notice a cannonball lodged in an upper wall of an outbuilding next door. The tour begins in the basement museum of the great house, a 1726 Georgian mansion that is said to be the oldest three-story brick home in Virginia. We watch a video about the plantation and then head up to the main floor to learn more about the place.

The first bourbon whisky was distilled here in 1621, and each of the first 10 U.S. presidents visited here, though those facts are not believed to have been related. After the Civil War, the Harrisons never regained the house, and it fell into disrepair. A former drummer boy among McClelland's troops, John Jamieson, returned in 1907 and purchased the plantation and set about restoring the home. His descendants still own Berkeley, and it remains a working plantation.

After the tour, guide Bessie Spence invites me to return for the annual reenactment of the first Thanksgiving, held here on the first Sunday of November. I make a note to come back.

For lunch, well, choices are limited along VA 5—other than SS Sub Shop, which is a dozen miles back up the road, there isn't much—which is why Charles City Tavern, 5 miles east of Berkeley, is such a nice surprise for travelers unfamiliar with the area. On the other hand, if you're willing to wait and you'd like lunch or dinner to be a bit of an adventure, you could drive another 25 miles to Jamestown, cross the river on the free Jamestown-Scotland Ferry that runs every half-hour in the summer and every hour in the fall and winter, and eat a bowl of peanut soup and a slice of peanut-raisin pie at The Surrey House Restaurant in the town of Surry, just across the river at the intersection of VA 31 and VA 10.

But we don't have the time today, which is not a problem because we get to stop instead at Charles City Tavern, a restored old house with a screen porch that's popular with diners. The tavern has become a destination for residents of Richmond, Williamsburg, and beyond. The food is great, and the atmosphere and friendly service match it. We're in a hurry to get to our next stop, Sherwood Forest, and we let our server know that, and she graciously hurries our order along. I choose the grilled tarragon chicken salad with red grapes and toasted pecans. It's terrific. My son orders a big bowl of the soup du jour, homemade tomato soup, and he runs out of adjectives praising it, which is saying something since he doesn't even think he *likes* tomato soup. We have no time or room for the chocolate bourbon

Sherwood Forest, the home of President John Tyler, stretches for 300 feet in length.

pecan pie or the molasses spice cake with warm caramel apples and vanilla ice cream, but I will another time.

East we go another 5 miles or so to Sherwood Forest, which like Shirley and Berkeley is on the right—the river side of the road. The grounds are open daily, but, unlike Shirley and Berkeley, the house is available for guided tours only by appointment. We have an appointment. We walk up through the circle of cedars lining the carriage driveway at the front of the house, and meet Tim Coyne, the plantation's genial caretaker.

Sherwood Forest was the home of John Tyler, the 10th U.S. president, who was the first vice president to ascend to the presidency due to the death of the president. In this case, he succeeded President William Henry Harrison, who died only a month after his inauguration. Harrison, of course, lived just up the river at Berkeley, but Tyler wasn't a neighbor at the time. He didn't purchase the plantation until 1842 when he was already in the White House, and he renamed it Sherwood Forest because of his reputation as a political outlaw. But here's what I find most interesting about Sherwood Forest: Tyler served as president from 1841 to 1845, and at the time of our visit his *grandson,* Harrison Tyler, still lives here. How? John Tyler fathered a son at age 63. That child fathered a son at age 75, in 1928. That son is Harrison Tyler.

Coyne tells us the home Sherwood Forest is the longest frame house in America, at just over 300 feet in length. The main portion of the house was constructed about 1720, but it has been added onto over the years, including a narrow ballroom John Tyler had built so he and his friends could dance the Virginia Reel in style and at home.

In Tyler's day, the river, more than a mile away, would have been visible from the house. Today, however, trees block the view. Coyne wants us to see the river, so he drives us a mile down the road to Fort Pocahontas, an earthen Civil War fort notable because it was built and maintained by black Union troops. The fort, near the river, lay forgotten and overgrown for more than a century until a military historian discovered it. Harrison Tyler purchased the land to preserve it for historical and archaeological research. He also opens it for group tours and annual reenactments.

Before going, we stop back by Sherwood Forest and walk through the cemetery for various Tyler pets through the years. We come upon a marker for John Tyler's favorite horse. It reads:

> Here lie the bones of my old horse, "General,"
>
> Who served his master faithfully
>
> For twenty-one years,
>
> And never made a blunder.
>
> Would that his master could say the same!

After a full afternoon, we thank Coyne, say goodbye, and head home. We return to the car and smile. We still have doughnuts.

IN THE AREA

Accommodations

Edgewood Plantation Bed and Breakfast, 4800 John Tyler Memorial Highway, Charles City. Call 804-829-2962. National Register of Historic Places. Web site: http://www.edgewoodplantation.com.

North Bend Plantation Bed and Breakfast, 12200 Weyanoke Road, Charles City. Call 804-829-5176. National Register of Historic Places. Web site: http://www.northbendplantation.com.

Piney Grove Bed and Breakfast at Southall's Plantation, 16920 Southall Plantation Lane, Charles City. Call 804-829-2916. National Register of Historic Places. Web site: http://www.pineygrove.com.

River's Rest Marina & Resort, 9100 Willcox Neck Road, Charles City. Call 804-829-2753. A 20-room motel overlooking the marina and the Chickahominy River. Web site: http://www.riversrest.com.

Attractions and Recreation

Berkeley Plantation, 12602 Harrison Landing Road, Charles City. Call 804-829-6018. Grounds and house open daily. Web site: http://www .berkeleyplantation.com.

Sherwood Forest Plantation, 14501 John Tyler Memorial Highway, Charles City. Call 804-829-5377. Grounds open daily, home tours by appointment. Web site: http://www.sherwoodforest.org.

Shirley Plantation, 501 Shirley Plantation Road, Charles City. Call 804-829-5121. Grounds and house open daily. Web site: http://www.shirley plantation.com.

Fort Pocahontas, 14501 John Tyler Memorial Highway, Charles City. Call 804-829-9722. Earthen Civil War fort. Tours by appointment. Web site: http://www.fortpocahontas.org.

Virginia Capital Trail. A 50-mile-long biking and walking trail connecting Richmond, Jamestown, and Williamsburg. Web site: http://www .virginiacapitaltrail.org.

Dining

Charles City Tavern, 9220 John Tyler Memorial Highway Charles City. Call: 804-829-5004. First-rate food, comfortable setting. Lunch and dinner. Web site: http://www.charlescitytavern.com.

Country Style Donuts, 4300 Williamsburg Road, Richmond. Call 804-222-2466. Great doughnuts. Open 24 hours a day.

SS Sub Shop, 19420 John Tyler Memorial Highway, Charles City. Call 804-829-9700. Burgers, hot dogs, sub sandwiches.

The Surrey House, 11865 Rolfe Highway, Surry. Call 757-294-3389. Country cooking, family dining. Web site: http://www.surreyhouse restaurant.com.

Other Contacts

Charles City Visitor Center, 10760 Courthouse Road Web site: http:// www.charlescity.org.

James River Plantations. Web site: http://www.jamesriverplantations .org.

Richmond National Battlefield Park, 3215 E. Broad Street, Richmond. Call 804-226-1981. Battlefields and forts along VA 5. Web site: http://www .nps.gov/rich.

Patrick Henry made his famous "Liberty or Death" speech at St. John's Church in Richmond.

CHAPTER

6

Road to Revolution

Patrick Henry gave voice to a rebellious cause

Estimated length: 50 miles
Estimated time: Day trip

Getting there: A logical starting point on the **Road to Revolution Heritage Trail** is historic **St. John's Church** in Richmond, 2401 E. Broad Street, where Patrick Henry delivered his famous "Give me liberty" speech in 1775. Then wind your way through suburbs and farmland across sprawling **Hanover County** to his home, **Scotchtown**, west of **Ashland**. If you have time, take another day and drive to **Red Hill,** in the foothills of the **Blue Ridge Mountains**, where Henry lived out his retirement and ultimately died and was buried.

Highlights: A tour of **St. John's Church** where reenactments of Henry's speech are held regularly. A visit to the site of **Historic Polegreen Church**, an unassuming spot that was a turning point for both Henry and the notion of religious freedom in America. A stop at the original **Hanover Courthouse**, one of the oldest in Virginia, and, right across the street, **Hanover Tavern**; once a way-station for travelers and now an intimate theater and restaurant. A meal at the tavern or next door at **Hanover Café**, or down the street at **Houndstooth Café**, or perhaps one of fine eateries in **Ashland**, the self-proclaimed "center of the universe" and a great little railroad town that maintains its All-American charm. A tour of **Scotchtown**

A young Patrick Henry argued one of his first major cases, the Parsons' Cause, at historic Hanover Courthouse.

completes the Richmond-area portion of the tour, though **Red Hill** beckons, 120 miles to the southwest.

When it comes to famous Virginia patriots during America's fight for independence, Patrick Henry sometimes gets lost amid the Washingtons, Jeffersons, and Adamses. But no one uttered more powerful words than Henry. "Give me liberty, or give me death," he said, and a fledgling nation seemed to listen.

"As you look at other patriots in the other colonies, it suddenly leaps out at you that Henry was active in what became the Revolution earlier than virtually anybody," says Jon Kukla, a historian and author who lived and worked as executive director at Red Hill, Henry's last home, and is writing a book on the role of Henry in the American Revolution. "He's near the center of events for the whole of the American founding. No other patriot—not Washington or Adams or Franklin—has that kind of presence."

Henry, a firebrand of a country lawyer from Hanover County, made his famous speech on March 23, 1775, standing in the boxed pews of Henrico Parish Church, site of the Second Virginia Convention. George Washington and Thomas Jefferson were among those in attendance.

Henrico Parish Church sat on Richmond Hill, a bluff overlooking the

James River and the docks and warehouses of the city. Decades later, the church's name was changed to St. John's, and the area became known as Church Hill. St. John's is the church in Church Hill. It's still there.

St. John's is a good place to start our journey. The steepled, white-frame church remains a well-visited historical site and home of an active Episcopal congregation. Built in 1741, the original church was plain with flat ceilings. The stained-glass windows and vaulted ceiling came later. Over the years, the church has been expanded around the original section, which still stands as the middle portion of the modern sanctuary.

The church property covers a square block and includes the oldest public cemetery in Richmond, along with several outbuildings, including a visitor center—a small brick structure that in the 1800s was a schoolhouse for neighborhood children. Church members buried in the churchyard include George Wythe, the first Virginian to sign the Declaration of Independence, and Elizabeth Arnold Poe, the mother of Edgar Allan Poe. By the way, the Poe Museum is only a half-mile away from St. John's, at 1914 E. Main Street.

You can wander around the grounds as long as you'd like—the grounds are open until 4 PM each day—or you might consider heading to the visitor center first. There, you can check out an exhibit about the church's history and Henry's era, and pay for a guided tour of the church and grounds.

Show up on a Sunday, and you can enjoy professional actors in period attire perform a reenactment of the Second Virginia Convention of 1775, culminating with Henry's speech. There's something about sitting in the old, wooden pews, listening to Henry's oratory that makes you want to arise when it's over and revolt. Although I guess we've already done that.

The free reenactments are held every Sunday afternoon in the summer, beginning Memorial Day through Labor Day weekend. The anniversary reenactment is held on the Sunday in March closest to March 23. Tours are offered daily.

Time to head away from the city toward Hanover County, a rambling combination of suburbia and bucolic countryside north of Richmond. Go west on Broad Street (US 250), down the hill from St. John's toward I-95 less than a mile away. Get on I-95 north for less than a mile and exit on I-64 east. Take US 360 east toward Mechanicsville (Exit 192) and follow that for 6.5 miles to Lee Davis Road and turn left. Go another 2 miles, then turn right on Pole Green Road. Go a half-mile to Rural Point Road and turn left, then another half-mile to Heatherwood Drive and turn right at a

Historic Polegreen Church celebrates the concept of religious freedom.

structure that looks like the white skeleton of a church. This is the site of Historic Polegreen Church.

The church is long gone, destroyed during the Civil War, but it wasn't so much the building that mattered but what happened here. Polegreen was one of the first meetinghouses of the "dissenter" movement in the 1700s against the Anglican Church, the only officially recognized religion in the colonies. A Presbyterian minister named Samuel Davies pastored the church during the 1750s. Davies is described as the first American-born hymn writer and is remembered for his pioneering and dangerous efforts to educate black slaves, but he might be best known as a peerless speaker. Two of his regular congregants were a young Patrick Henry and his mother. Henry has been quoted as crediting Davies for "teaching me what an orator should be."

Stroll along the walkway of brick and granite at Polegreen Church, a timeline that chronicles the history of the global struggle for religious freedom. The centerpiece of the site, of course, is the silhouette of the church—

a white frame with empty doorways, glass-less windows, and the outline of the roof—which makes for an arresting image. A visitor center is in the works, and the Historic Polegreen Church Foundation has acquired more than 100 acres surrounding the site so that it will be preserved from development—and its offerings expanded—for the years to come. Polegreen Church is an example of great local history with national implications.

"I think that's a great way to put it," says Christopher K. Peace, executive director of Historic Polegreen Church Foundation, and a member of the Virginia House of Delegates from Hanover who introduced the legislation in the General Assembly that established the Road to Revolution trail. "We take for granted the First Amendment and religious freedom. We're very proud the movement for that started here."

This area is Henry's stomping grounds. He was born nearby at Studley Plantation, but there's nothing there now but a bean field. He was married at a home called Rural Plains. The home, on Studley Road just south of Rural Point Road, was in private hands for generations, but has been acquired by the National Park Service. It eventually will be open to the public.

From Polegreen Church, I follow Rural Point Road west to US 301, a pretty 4-mile drive past wooded neighborhoods and farms, and then turn right and head north on US 301. In about 7 miles, I will come to Hanover Courthouse, but before that I reach Hanover Wayside, a 36-acre park that's perfect for a picnic and also features the Hanover Veterans Memorial. I also pass a Shell gas station at Stumpy Road where I see a historic marker for the birthplace of Henry Clay. He didn't spend a lot of time in Hanover before moving west, but he and Patrick Henry are considered the most famous historical figures to come out of the county.

At Hanover Courthouse, I find the county's government complex, as well as a couple of historic buildings—the original courthouse and Hanover Tavern—and several good places to eat.

Built in 1735, the courthouse is another Henry stop, the place where as a young, obscure lawyer he spoke eloquently against King George III in the Parsons' Cause, a political dispute viewed by some as a foreshadowing of the revolution. The courthouse is open weekly, and reenactments are held periodically.

Hanover Tavern is a local gem, a 200-year-old landmark and longtime way station for travelers that now houses a full-service restaurant and Barksdale Theatre, an intimate theater for professional productions.

If you have the time, by all means stay for a show. I've been attending plays there for 30 years, and it's always a treat.

Next door to the tavern is Hanover Café, a pleasant place with wooden booths and a view of the old courthouse across the street. I meet Chris Peace for lunch. He orders the chicken salad sandwich; I get the Hanover Club. Both are excellent. Just down the road, at the corner of US 301 and VA 54, is the Houndstooth Café, another local favorite known for its splendid food.

Peace grew up in Ashland and lives in Mechanicsville—Hanover's two largest towns—so he knows this area and loves it. I ask him to describe Hanover for someone who might not be familiar with it.

"It's a great county," says Peace. "People here have always been united around its heritage and history. The spirit of liberty really resounds here. We're a Mayberry kind of place. Some of that small town USA still lives here, and I think that makes us a unique place in the middle of suburban sprawl of the capital region. I think our history has helped us keep that sense of place and community."

Besides following the Road to Revolution Heritage Trail, Peace suggests visitors tour the county's Civil War battlefields, such as Cold Harbor, stop by Mechanicsville or Ashland, attend the Ashland Strawberry Faire each June, and the Hanover Tomato Festival each July. The county is well known for its Hanover tomatoes.

Hanover Tavern is home to a full-service restaurant and Barksdale Theatre

I head to Ashland, turning left from US 301 onto VA 54 and going west, through woods and past farmland and some of the most handsome homes you might hope to see anywhere. I cross I-95 and reach Ashland, which is home to Randolph-Macon College, a rail line that runs right through the middle of town, and the good-humored nickname: Center of the Universe.

Regardless of the town's placement in the universe, this is a fine place to be if you're hungry, with offerings such as the Ironhorse Restaurant, which describes its menu as "seasonal, Southern modern American" and which I describe as just plain good, and Homemades by Suzanne, which has about the best salads and sandwiches anywhere and desserts to match. There's also Ashland Coffee & Tea, a popular hangout because of its wireless Internet and its live music, as well as its coffee, tea, and snacks. The Smokey Pig, a casual barbecue place over on US 1, is another local favorite.

You can watch the big trains go by, or the small ones at Train Town Toy & Hobby, in the same block as the Ironhorse. Or wander over to Ashland Feed Store and chat up its owner, Danny Adams, or some of the locals who gather there to discuss the local corn crop or to solve the world's ills or both. It's a friendly, throwback kind of place with sacks of seed and feed, as well as a cooler of Grape and Orange Nehi sodas.

Scotchtown, Henry's plantation home during the 1770s, is 11 miles west of Ashland on VA 54, a lovely country road. Henry and his wife, Sarah, and their six children lived at Scotchtown. Henry rode from Scotchtown to Richmond to deliver his "Give me liberty" speech, and in 1776, he was elected governor. By then, tragedy had visited his family. Sarah Henry began showing signs of mental illness around the time they moved to Scotchtown. She apparently was confined to a basement room at Scotchtown before dying in 1775. Henry remarried in 1777 and moved to Williamsburg when he was elected Virginia's first governor. Scotchtown is open to the public Friday through Sunday much of the year.

Scotchtown is the end of my trip, but if you have the time, there are two additional suggested sites that are more far-flung along the Road to Revolution tour: Hampden-Sydney College, the 10th-oldest college in the United States that Henry helped establish in 1775, and Red Hill, in Brookneal, his final home and resting place. Both are in south-central Virginia, about 100 miles from Ashland. Red Hill was a thriving tobacco plantation in Henry's day. Today, you can walk the quiet grounds, visit a reconstruction of Henry's modest home—a museum with a large collection of Henry memorabilia—and see the cemetery where he is buried. His tombstone reads: HIS FAME HIS BEST EPITAPH.

IN THE AREA

Accommodations

Henry Clay Inn, 114 N. Railroad Avenue, Ashland. Country inn, which opened in 1992 but is a replica of earlier inns in the area. Offers 14 guest rooms, a restaurant, and an art and gift gallery featuring the works of local artists. Web site: http://www.henryclayinn.com.

Attractions and Recreation

Hanover Tavern, 13181 Hanover Courthouse Road, Hanover. Call 804-537-5050. Web site: http://www.hanovertavern.org.

Historic Polegreen Church, 6411 Heatherwood Drive, Mechanicsville. Call 804-730-3837. Church where the Reverend Samuel Davies, a Presbyterian minister and leader of the dissenter movement, preached. The young Patrick Henry and his mother were among his regular congregation. Web site: http://www.historicpolegreen.org.

Red Hill, the Patrick Henry National Memorial, 1250 Red Hill Road, Brookneal. Call 434-376-2044. Patrick Henry lived his final years here and is buried here. Web site: http://www.redhill.org.

Rural Plains, 7273 Studley Road, Mechanicsville. Call 804-226-1981. Site of Patrick Henry's first marriage and also site of the Civil War battle of Totopotomy Creek. Web site: http://www.nps.gov/rich.

St. John's Episcopal Church, 2401 E. Broad Street, Richmond. Call 804-648-5015. Site of Patrick Henry's "Give me liberty" speech. An active church open for tours and reenactments. Web site: www.historicstjohns church.org.

Scotchtown, 16120 Chiswell Lane, Beaverdam. Call 804-227-3500. Home of Patrick Henry during the period when he gave his "Give me liberty" speech and when he was elected governor. Web site: http://www.apva.org /scotchtown.

Dining

Ashland Coffee & Tea, 100 N. Railroad Avenue, Ashland. Call 804-798-1702. Comfortable coffee shop with wireless Internet and live music. Web site: http://www.ashlandcoffeeandtea.com.

Hanover Café, 13185 Hanover Courthouse Road, Hanover. Call 804-537-5290. Breakfast, lunch, and dinner. Good, basic food. Reasonable prices. Web site: http://www.hanovercafe.nv.switchboard.com.

Homemades By Suzanne, 102 N. Railroad Avenue, Ashland. Call 804-798-8331. Fresh sandwiches and salads, exquisite desserts, and boxed lunches. Web site: http://www.homemadesbysuzanne.com.

Houndstooth Café, 13271 Hanover Courthouse Road, Hanover. Call 804-537-5404. Web site: http://billofare.com/1404.htm.

Ironhorse Restaurant, 100 S. Railroad Avenue, Ashland. Call 804-752-6410. Inviting corner restaurant on the town's rail line that's a combination upscale bistro and neighborhood pub. Live music. Web site: http://www.ironhorserestaurant.com.

The Smokey Pig, 212 S. Washington Highway (US 1), Ashland. Call 804-798-4590. Housed in a former general store, restaurant specializes in barbecue, and also serves burgers, sandwiches, and other Southern-style fare. Web site: http://www.thesmokeypig.com.

Other Contacts

Civil War Trails. Web site: http://www.civilwartraveler.com.

Parsons' Cause Foundation, P.O. Box 364, Mechanicsville. Visit http://www.parsonscause.org.

Road to Revolution Heritage Trail, Richmond Metropolitan Convention and Visitor Bureau, 401 N. 3rd Street, Richmond. Call 1-888-742-4666. Web site: http://www.roadtorevolution.org.

Town of Ashland, 101 Thompson Street, Ashland. Call 804-798-9212. Web site: http://www.town.ashland.va.us.

Brunswick County is home to a historic courthouse and Brunswick Stew

CHAPTER

7

The Longest Road

At more than 500 miles, US 58 is a daunting drive, but here's a tasty sampling

Estimated length: 150 miles
Estimated time: Day trip

Getting there: Start at **Emporia** at I-95, Exit 11, and US 58, and head west on US 58 to **Martinsville.**

Highlights: An easy drive, this section of **US 58** unspools through the rolling farmland of Southside Virginia, along its border with North Carolina, and connects a series of small towns and cities—nearly forgotten places such as **Boydton**, among others—trying to find their economic way following the decline of the textile and tobacco industries. If you're lucky, you'll find a fresh bowl of **Brunswick Stew** from a massive, steaming pot at a fire department fundraiser, or drop by the **Cinnamon Café** in **Lawrenceville** and order it from the menu any day. If you time your visit right, you can hit the **Virginia Pork Festival** in **Emporia** in June or the **Virginia Cantaloupe Festival** near **South Boston** every July. The **Tobacco Farm Life Museum of Virginia** in **South Hill**, and the **Virginia Museum of Natural History** in **Martinsville**. **Lake Gaston**, a 20,000-acre, man-made lake along the Virginia-North Carolina border is a haven for boating, fishing, and skiing enthusiasts. Racing? There's **Virginia International Raceway** near Danville, one of the finest road courses in the world, and **Martinsville Speedway** has the longest history and the shortest track in NASCAR history.

US 58 is a much different road than it used to be. Once a two-lane road snaking through rural Virginia along its southern border, US 58 was a death trap in many areas where the pavement was narrow, shoulders were thin, and impatient motorists foolishly tried passing slower vehicles. Fed up with horrific crashes and unnecessary deaths, Greensville County even erected a sign along the road in the 1980s: CAUTION: APPROACHING SUICIDE STRIP.

But those days are gone. In recent decades, US 58, in many stretches where mountains or creeks don't get in the way, has been straightened and widened to a four-lane divided highway, a veritable mini-interstate that extends more than 500 miles from Virginia Beach in the east to Cumberland Gap, the westernmost point in the state. The distance becomes almost 600 miles if you throw in US 58-Alternate that branches off at Abingdon and curls through Coeburn and Big Stone Gap in the far southwest, before once again joining the mother road at Jonesville.

Yet, the tradeoff for the safety and comfort of a fine highway is that you can miss much of the region's charm and history by bypassing the little towns that grew up along the old road. So, plan to veer off the main highway and detour through the towns. The "business route" versions of US 58 seldom last more than a couple of miles, and you never know what you'll find: an inviting little diner, a small museum, or maybe an antiques shop with a hidden treasure.

Start at Emporia, an hour's drive south of Richmond, developed as a hub of commerce at the junction of two railroads, as well as its location at the intersection of US 58 and first US 301 and then I-95. Emporia is home of the Virginia Pork Festival, held on the second Wednesday of every June since the 1970s. The festival highlights the region's pork production and features barbecued spareribs, minced barbecue, sausage biscuits, ham biscuits, country-fried ham and red eye gravy, loin chops, pigs feet, pork burgers, BLTs, and, well, you get the idea. The chitterlings, I will advise you, are an acquired taste. The sweet tea and the beer are always cold, and the hush puppies and French fried sweet potatoes are very good, too. Festival organizers prepare more than 43,000 pounds of pork each year, but attendance is limited to 15,000, so order your tickets ahead of time.

Going west from Emporia, you'll drive through one of the best-named places anywhere: Pleasant Shade. But don't blink. Like a lot of small communities along US 58, Pleasant Shade was once a railroad depot. Now that the depot's gone, Pleasant Shade is little more than a few homes, a general store, and a Baptist church. But it still looks pretty pleasant.

If you'd like to explore US 58 east of Emporia, you have numerous options. In a 60-mile stretch, you will come to **Courtland**, **Franklin**, and **Suffolk**, and then the **Great Dismal Swamp Wildlife Refuge**. Farther east, and you start getting into the seamless sprawl that leads into Norfolk and Virginia Beach.

In Courtland, on US 58-Business, stop by the small but first-rate **Rawls Museum Arts**, a partner of the Virginia Museum of Fine Arts that focuses on regional and emerging artists. The outdoor displays at the **Southampton Agriculture & Forestry Museum and Heritage Village** will take you back in time. As long as you're in one of the premier peanut-producing regions in the world, you might as well sample the famous local product. Pay a visit to **The Peanut Patch**, on US 58, or one of the other peanut shops in the area.

Just east of Courtland, you will come upon Franklin, a town wrestling with the loss of its primary industry, a local paper mill that announced in 2009 it would close down its operations. Generations of families have worked at the mill, its smokestacks rising just across the **Blackwater River** from the town. Drive through Franklin's pretty residential area, handsome homes along wide, leafy avenues. The downtown area, hit hard by floodwaters in years past, already was spotty with boarded up businesses, but grab a bite at **Fred's Restaurant** or **Parker Drug Co**., both favorite local hangouts.

Suffolk is the largest city in Virginia in terms of land size, created from a 1970s merger of the old town of Suffolk and former Nansemond County and covering more than 430 square miles. Much of the area remains rural, although it has become a suburb of Norfolk and Virginia Beach to the east. Suffolk developed around the peanut industry, specifically **Planters Peanuts**, and in the town's historic district you'll find statues and other tributes to Mr. Peanut, the company's iconic symbol. The state's annual **Peanut Fest** is held in Suffolk for four days each October, attracting an estimated 200,000.

One place you might not, on first thought, consider visiting but ought to is the **Great Dismal Swamp National Wildlife Refuge.** The swamp, whose northern edge reaches US 58 just east of Suffolk, includes more than 110,000 acres of forested wetlands in Virginia and North Carolina. The centerpiece is 3,100-acre **Lake Drummond.** The swamp is a rich habitat for all sorts of critters and can be spooky at night, but it's a beautiful and fascinating place to visit. Just make sure you stick to the designated trails because it's easy to get lost if you wander into the dense woods. I've walked the trails, which are narrow unpaved roads originally constructed for timber access, but the most popular trail is the **Washington Ditch Boardwalk Trail,** which makes swamp exploration a lot more civilized and accessible. And if you go in the spring or fall, the mosquitoes aren't bad at all.

Ten miles west of Pleasant Shade, leave the bypass and take the old road into Lawrenceville, the seat of Brunswick County, home of Brunswick Stew, a local dish that dates back, legend has it, to the 1800s. The General Assembly of Virginia even passed a resolution proclaiming Brunswick County as the "original home of Brunswick Stew." It's made with chicken now—instead of the original squirrel—but Brunswick Stew remains a favorite meal around Virginia and a great way to raise money for charity and other worthy causes.

"During the fall and winter, there is a pot of stew being cooked in this county just about every weekend," says John D. Clary, president of Brunswick Box Co. and a certified Stew Master who in his spare time cooks hundreds of quarts of stew at a time for schools, churches, and the local volunteer fire department, among other organizations.

I've been privileged to witness Clary and his buddies cooking giant caldrons of stew, and then taste the results. All I can say is, it's pure nectar.

If you don't run into a stew sale or can't make the annual Taste of Brunswick Festival on the second Saturday in October at Southside Virginia Community College, you can always stop by a place like The Cinnamon Café, where they serve stew as a menu item, or you can have it shipped frozen. But the café, across the street from the sort of stately county courthouse you'd expect to find in a Southern town, offers a broad menu, as well as WiFi. As we drive through town, we're in the mood for pizza and e-mail, so we stop and get both at the café, as well as very good service.

Downtown Lawrenceville, once a thriving center of commerce with a department store and a drug store in the same block with the courthouse, has lost both and is in transition. One thing Lawrenceville hasn't lost is its history, which you can explore at the Brunswick County Museum on Courthouse Square or in the courthouse itself. Brunswick, once a vast county covering much of southern Virginia, was one of the rare places in the South not to have its records destroyed during the Civil War. It has records dating to the 1700s and is a popular destination for genealogical researchers.

Lake Rawlings is a little out of the way but an interesting diversion. Twenty miles north of Lawrenceville off VA 46 and US 1, Lake Rawlings is an old quarry, filled by spring water; it is a popular destination for scuba divers from all over the country. Advertised as "the clearest lake from Maine to Florida," Lake Rawlings has a maximum depth of 65 feet and good visibility, plus attractions such as sunken buses and planes to dive to. Camping is available on-site.

Back on US 58, 15 miles west of Lawrenceville we come to South Hill. The road crosses I-85 and US 1 here, so you have a full selection of fast-food restaurants, motels, and gas stations, but if you venture off the main highway onto the business route again, you'll come to a town with shops and restaurants. In the heart of town, you'll find the restored railroad depot, now housing the local chamber of commerce as well as the South Hill Model Railroad Museum and the Virginia S. Evans Doll Museum. The railroad museum features a sprawling reproduction of the Atlantic and Danville Railroad. The painstakingly handmade exhibit took seven years to construct, plus a lot of green fiber, toothpicks, and hairspray.

A block away, you might want to stop at the Tobacco Farm Life Museum, since this town grew up with the tobacco industry and was a central point in tobacco sale and production, with a half-dozen tobacco warehouses. Today, the industry is a shadow of its former self. The museum, in a triangle-shaped brick structure because it sat on the corner with railroad tracks running behind it, doesn't so much memorialize the plant on which Virginia was built but pays tribute to the farm families who grew the labor-intensive crop.

Hungry? Wilson's BBQ, featuring country barbecue, country cooking, and homemade pies, is a popular spot. It's on the west side of town and always seems to be busy and its parking lot crowded.

West of South Hill, the terrain gently rises and falls, and US 58 stretches into the distance across the undulating hills. Another 15 miles, past fields of soybeans and other crops, brings you to Boydton, a town that's been rebounding for a lot of years. In 1977, *U.S. News & World Report* wrote a story about Boydton and described it as "a small town that refuses to die."

The town used to be a bustling center of commerce with hardware stores, an automobile dealership, and a grocery, but they've been gone for years, the victims of a struggling economy in a region dependent on tobacco and manufacturing. The construction of the US 58 bypass further hastened the town's decline. But recent construction signals a comeback, starting with the restoration and expansion of the handsome Mecklenburg County courthouse, the town's centerpiece that's modeled on the state capitol in Richmond.

The town has undergone a facelift with new sidewalks and streetlights and rehabbed storefronts. An impressive new medical center takes up an entire block, and historic Boyd Tavern, an 18th-century center for food and lodging, has been restored and is open for tours. Willow Grove Marina, a new marina with 135 boat slips, provides easy access to Buggs Island Lake, which is just down the road. We stop by Bill Thompson's Olde Lamps & Thangs, an antique shop just west of the town center, and stroll among the treasures he's found or fixed up. You can get good strombolis, pizza, and other Itailan dishes at Rose's, a small restaurant across from the courthouse. If you're staying the night, the Southern Heritage Bed & Breakfast is a fine option.

Mayor Bob Salzmann, a transplanted New Yorker, tells me things are looking up for the town and it could be booming again before long.

"This town is definitely refusing to die," he says.

Continuing west on US 58 takes you across the northern edge of Buggs Island Lake, the state's largest lake with 50,000 acres of water and 800 miles of shoreline. Before Clarksville you might consider a stop at Occoneechee State Park, which is on the lake; it features 18 miles of trails to explore, a vis-

A new US 58 bridge is but one mode of transportation at Clarksville, a gateway to Buggs Island Lake.

itor center depicting the history of the Occoneechee Indians, and grounds that portray plantation life in the 1800s.

US 58 now bypasses Clarksville with a gleaming bridge across the lake, but, like other towns along the road, Clarksville is well worth a stop. The town's downtown area, focused along old US 58, has brick-lined sidewalks and numerous shops and restaurants in buildings that date back to the 18th century. The big event in Clarksville is the Virginia Lake Festival every July that attracts more than 80,000 visitors.

Less than 20 miles west of Clarksville brings you to South Boston, where you come into a historic tobacco and factory town, where the whistle at the old Halifax Cotton Mill used to blow at 7 o'clock every morning to call the town to work. You can glimpse that past at the South Boston-Halifax County Museum of Fine Arts and History. If you're around town in July, you can head over to the Halifax County Fairgrounds for the annual Virginia Cantaloupe Festival, where you can have a good time and a half of a cantaloupe, scooped out and filled with vanilla ice cream. Mighty good. If you're not around for the festival, a good place for an ice cream stop any time is Dairy Dell, a tiny drive-in on US 58, just east of US 501. I always stop for one of the Dell's great milk shakes when I'm driving through South Boston, as I do on this trip. You can get hot dogs and other food, too.

Danville, an old tobacco and textile city, is next up, more than 30 miles west of South Boston. But before you get to Danville, if you're an automobile or motorcycle racing fan, you might want to turn off US 58 on VA 62, go briefly into North Carolina, and then back into Virginia to find Virginia International Raceway, a world-class road course hidden away on the southern banks of the Dan River. If speed's your game, you don't want to miss this place.

If you follow the US 58 bypass signs, you will miss Danville completely, going south along the North Carolina border, before re-emerging on the west side of Danville. To see Danville, you need to follow old US 58 through town; to truly see Danville, you need to get off US 58 entirely and go south across the Dan River. There you will find the historic mill district, which offers a number of restaurants and shops, as well as the Danville Science Center, a division of the Science Museum of Virginia, housed in the 1899 Southern Railway Passenger Station. The stunning butterfly garden is a focal point of the science center. Next door is the Danville Farmers' Market, held every Saturday morning, year-round.

One of Danville's claims to fame is that one of its homes was the last capitol of the Confederacy. After Confederate President Jefferson Davis fled Richmond at the end of the Civil War he set up the government—for a week—in the Danville home of Major William Sutherlin. The Sutherlin Mansion, situated along a lovely stretch of Main Street featuring large homes and historic churches, is now home to the Danville Museum of Fine Arts and History, well worth a visit. The upstairs bedroom occupied by Davis has been restored.

A highlight of Martinsville, 20 miles west of Danville, is the Virginia Museum of Natural History, a top-notch museum made all the better when it moved into a new facility in 2007. Another is Martinsville Speedway, the shortest track on the Sprint Cup circuit and the only one to have hosted a major NASCAR race since its inception in 1949.

IN THE AREA

Accommodations

Brunswick Mineral Springs Bed & Breakfast, 14910 Western Mill Road, Lawrenceville. Call 1-888-723-7567. Rooms decorated with period antiques. Country breakfast. Gourmet dinner. Nature trails on the 28-acre estate. Web site: http://www.brunswickmineralsprings.com.

Southern Heritage Bed & Breakfast, 1100 Jefferson Street, Boydton. Call 434-738-0167. Queen Anne Victorian home built in 1880 with wrap-around porch and Southern touches. Web site: http://www.bbonline.com /va/southern.

Attractions and Recreation

Danville Museum of Fine Arts and History, 975 Main Street, Danville. Call 434-793-5644. Sutherlin Mansion also served as last capitol of the Confederacy. Web site: http://www.danvillemuseum.org.

Danville Science Center, 677 Craghead Street, Danville. Call 434-791-5160. A division of the Science Museum of Virginia, housed in a railroad station. Web site: http://www.dsc.smv.org.

The Danville home that served as the last capitol of the Confederacy is now a museum of fine arts and history

Great Dismal Swamp Wildlife Refuge, 3100 Desert Road, Suffolk. Call 757-986-3705. Hiking, biking, and exploring nature. Web site: http://www.fws.gov/northeast/greatdismalswamp.

Lake Rawlings, One Quarry Lane, Rawlings. Call 804-478-9000. Scuba diving and camping park. Web site: http://www.lakerawlings.com.

Rawls Museum Arts, 22376 Linden Street, Courtland. Call 757-653-0754. Art gallery and museum. Web site: http://www.rawlsarts.com.

Virginia Cantaloupe Festival, P.O. Box 399, South Boston. Call 1-888-458-1003. A celebration of the melon on a Friday evening each July. Web site: http://www.valopefest.com.

Virginia International Raceway, 1245 Pine Tree Road, Alton. Call 434-822-7700. World-class road course for races, driving schools, and private testing. Web site: http://www.virnow.com.

Virginia Museum of Natural Resources, 21 Starling Avenue, Martinsville. Call 276-634-4141. Interprets Virginia's natural history. Web site: http://www.vmnh.net.

Virginia Pork Festival, 425 South Main Street, Emporia. Call 434-634-6611. Second Wednesday every June. Web site: http://www.vaporkfestival .com.

Dining

Cinnamon Café, 229 N. Main Street, Lawrenceville. Call 434-848-2226. Wide-ranging, reasonably priced menu, including Brunswick Stew, which is available for mail order. Web site: http://www.thecinnamoncafe.com.

Dairy Dell, 1041 Bill Tuck Highway (US 58), South Boston. Call 434-572-8245. Best milk shakes in town. Drive-in fare.

Rose's Pizza Restaurant, 109 Bank Street, Boydton. Call 434-738-9500. Pizzas, strombolis, cheesesteaks, and a variety of Italian dishes.

Other Contacts

Boydton, 461 Madison Street, Boydton. Call 434-738-6344. Web site: http://www.boydton.org.

Brunswick County Tourism, 228 N. Main Street, Lawrenceville. Call 1-866-783-9768. Web site: http://www.tourbrunswick.org.

Danville Tourism, 645 River Park Drive, Danville. Call 434-793-4636. Web site: http://www.visitdanville.com.

Martinsville and Henry County Chamber of Commerce, P.O. Box 709, Martinsville. Call 276-632-6401. Web site: http://www.mhcchamber .com.

South Hill Chamber of Commerce, 201 South Mecklenburg Avenue, South Hill. Call 434-447-4547. Web site: http://www.southhillchamber .com.

Tobacco Heritage Trails, 200 Harrison Street, LaCrosse. Call 434-757-7438. A developing rails-to-trails bicycling and walking trail in the US 58 corridor of Southern Virginia. Web site: http://www.tobaccoheritage trail.org.

A wax figure of a 45-year-old George Washington at Valley Forge appears at the Donald W. Williams Museum and Education Center at George Washington's Mt. Vernon: Estate & Gardens. MOUNT VERNON LADIES' ASSOCIATION

CHAPTER

8

By George

In search of the real Washington, and, of course, cherry pie

Estimated length: 90 miles
Estimated time: 2 days

Getting there: From I-95, go east on VA 3 (near Fredericksburg) for 35 miles to VA 204. Turn left and follow signs to George Washington Birthplace National Monument. The trip continues back to Fredericksburg, and then north on US 1 to Mt. Vernon and Alexandria.

Highlights: Begin at **George Washington Birthplace National Monument**, then proceed to **Ferry Farm** near Fredericksburg where Washington spent his childhood, and then north to **Mt. Vernon** where Washington lived much of his adult life, when he wasn't fighting in the Revolutionary War or serving as America's first president. Spend the night in the vibrant **Old Town** district of **Alexandria**, a city Washington surveyed and often visited. With enough time, you can also stop by **Stratford Hall**, Robert E. Lee's birthplace, picnic, or kayak the **Potomac River** at **Westmoreland State Park**, and sip Chardonnay at **Ingleside Vineyards.**

Let's get this straight: George Washington probably never chopped down a cherry tree and then readily confessed the act to his father, but the Mt. Vernon Inn Restaurant serves a killer cherry pie. Which just proves it doesn't matter whether a story is true as long as the desserts are good.

We start where he was born in 1732, a pretty piece of land wedged between Popes Creek and the Potomac River, preserved now as the George Washington Birthplace National Monument. Off the beaten path and not named Mt. Vernon, it's unknown to many Virginians. I've lived in the commonwealth most of my life, and this is my first visit.

"This is one of the best-kept secrets in Virginia," said Rijk Morawe, Natural and Cultural Resources Program Manager at the park.

Part of the reason the birthplace remains off the radar for many is that Washington lived here only the first three and a half years of his life, the park is 45 minutes from the nearest interstate highway, and, frankly, there is little here that physically ties him to it. Except, simply walking the grounds, reading the historical notes, and hearing the stories of how generations of Washingtons settled this place lends a realness to the early years of a man whose life has grown to mythical proportions.

At the visitor center, we browse through the exhibits and come upon something I did not know: Washington was born, not on February 22, but on February 11—according to the Julian calendar that was followed in the British colonies in the early 1700s. When Great Britain switched to the Gregorian calendar in 1752, an adjustment in number of days meant Washington's birthday would now be celebrated on February 22.

Down a path through a grove of towering junipers, we come to the site of the home where Washington was born. Crushed oyster shells mark the outline of the foundation of a modest home, unearthed and then covered up again by archaeologists. Perhaps 100 feet away, we see the Memorial House, a fine, brick home constructed in the 1930s that is open for touring, and typical of the upper classes of that period but probably nicer than the Washingtons' home. Costumed interpreters do a nice job of connecting the Washingtons to the land and the period, putting into context the era into which the "father of his country" was born.

George's great-grandfather, John, settled the area for the Washingtons, immigrating to America in the 1650s. A successful planter and member of the Virginia House of Burgesses, he foreshadowed his great-grandson's love of farming and public service. The family burial ground, the final resting place for many of George's relatives except himself (he is buried at Mt. Vernon), is near the original John Washington home site. It's also on the road to the park's small beach, which we stroll along for a short distance.

We eat the lunch we brought at the park's picnic area and then walk it off on the mile-long nature trail that loops around by Popes Creek.

As long as you're here, you might not want to miss Stratford Hall, home of the Lee family and not more than a 10-minute drive east on VA 3 to VA 214. Make a left on VA 214 and then travel 2 miles to the **Stratford Hall** entrance.

Richard Henry Lee and Francis Lightfoot Lee, the only brothers to sign the Declaration of Independence, grew up here, as did Robert E. Lee, who led Confederate forces in the Civil War. Henry "Lighthorse Harry" Lee, Robert's father, famously eulogized George Washington with, "First in war, first in peace, and first in the hearts of his countrymen."

Stratford Hall was built in the 1730s, a magnificent brick home, particularly considering the limited tools and materials available at the time. The home is open daily for tours, as is the 1,900-acre plantation, which features an exquisite garden, a working farm, and a splendid view of the river from the property's high bluffs. There's also a visitor center with informative exhibits about the Lees and a dining room that specializes in Southern cooking. You can even make arrangements to stay at the plantation in a guest house or cabin.

Next door to Stratford Hall, less than a mile down VA 3, is **Westmoreland State Park**, on a picturesque stretch of the Potomac that is perfect for boating, hiking, and picnicking. For overnight stays, the park offers cabins, lodges, and a campground.

Kayaking tops the list of favorite activities at Westmoreland State Park on the Potomac River.

Feel like a taste (or two) of wine? Take VA 3 toward Fredericksburg, and when you come to Oak Grove, go south on VA 638 for two miles to **Ingleside Vineyards**, one of the wineries that helped jump-start the Virginia wine industry when it opened in the 1970s. Carl Flemer, a longtime dairy farmer on the highest piece of land on The Neck, the strip of land between the Potomac and Rappahannock rivers, transformed a portion of his property into a vineyard. His son, Doug, now runs the place, which produces 15,000 cases of wine a year, and offers wine-tastings. It almost goes without saying that all of the Ingleside wines I have sampled are excellent, but you can't beat the popular (and reasonably priced) Blue Crab label.

If you have the time and inclination to visit **Colonial Beach**, head back to VA 3 but keep straight through the intersection onto VA 205 and drive 6 miles to the once-thriving resort on the Potomac that's making a comeback. Colonial Beach has not only a busy beach, but a state-champion cherrybark oak–yes, there are such competitions—that at more than 100 feet in height dwarfs the one-story home at 215 Ball Street, only a few blocks from the beach. If you're hungry or feeling lucky, try the **Riverboat on the Potomac**, a restaurant and off-track betting parlor that looks like a riverboat and extends from the shore into the river. Oh, and rent a golf cart. A designated "golf cart town," Colonial Beach permits licensed drivers to operate carts on its roads.

On to Fredericksburg, where we visit Ferry Farm, Washington's boyhood home, on the banks of the Rappahannock. Ferry Farm is on VA 3, about 30 miles from Oak Grove. Its entrance is slightly hidden and requires a U-turn, traveling from the east. Just remember it's just past where VA 3 goes to the left and VA 3-Business keeps straight. You keep straight. Ferry Farm will be on your left, not more than a few hundred yards ahead.

If Washington chopped any cherry trees, this is where he would have done it. Same with the story about him tossing a silver dollar across the Potomac. That's not true for a couple of reasons, according to officials at Mt. Vernon Estate and Gardens: there were no silver dollars when Washington was a young man and the Potomac is about a mile wide. Washington, according to his step-grandson, threw a piece of slate across the Rappahannock, which, where it passes Ferry Farm, is a more manageable 250 feet or so across. I pick up a few rocks, give it all I've got, and each goes *kerplunk* about halfway across the river. All I prove is I'm no George Washington, and now my arm's sore, too.

We arrive late in the afternoon at Ferry Farm, so we do a quick tour of the 80-acre property: small museum, nature trails, archaeology work that has revealed the site of the Washington home. George swam in the river and rode the ferry, which stopped just below the farm, to Fredericksburg. He learned to grow tobacco, wheat, and corn here, and took up surveying. He grew into manhood. After his father's death in 1743, George spent less and less time at the farm, often visiting his half-brother, Lawrence, at his place at Little Hunting Creek, which later became known as Mt. Vernon.

That's where we are heading eventually. Mt. Vernon is about an hour's drive north. If you aren't in a hurry, take US 1, the Mother Road of the East Coast in its heyday. Anyone of a certain age who did any traveling along the Eastern Seaboard in the days before interstate highways will remember the old-style motels and the kitschy tourist attractions along the road. Most of the just-passing-through traffic crowds I-95, but US 1 is far from a barren landscape. Quite the contrary, in many stretches the road is wall-to-wall businesses, and the going is sometimes quite slow, between the traffic and the traffic lights. But it's worth a look.

We will save a closer look at Fredericksburg for another trip, but it too is deserving of an extensive visit for, among other reasons, the University of Mary Washington, named for George's mother, and its numerous Civil War sites. In fact, if you want a one-of-a-kind Civil War museum experience, pay a visit to the White Oak Civil War Museum.

You'll find the museum 6 miles east of Fredericksburg on VA 218 (known locally as White Oak Road) in a renovated school house. The place is filled with thousands of relics—buckles, bullets, and bottles, as well as weapons, tools, and coins—many of them found by D. P. Newton and his father, Patrick, in nearby fields and woods that were wartime camps, Union and Confederate. D. P. Newton, an unassuming man and amateur historian who has painstakingly arranged and identified the artifacts, poured his savings into setting up White Oak. Charles F. Bryan Jr., retired chief executive officer of the Virginia Historical Society, tells me it's "one of the most remarkable museums I've ever seen."

Newton also has drawn detailed maps of the wartime camps he's excavated since he was a child—many of them now covered by modern development—and constructed replicas of soldiers' huts and even a cannon. Newton purchased the old White Oak School, which he attended as a child, and converted it into the museum, although he kept the potbellied stove and chalkboards. The museum is well off the favored tourist routes, but

Newton has had visitors from all over the United States, Europe, and Asia.

If you're craving a quick bite, try Allman's Bar-B-Q, a landmark on US 1 in Fredericksburg. It's nothing fancy: a small brick building, with a few tables, a counter—and Mom, Mary Elizabeth Brown, the effervescent queen of the kitchen who's been using her well-guarded secret recipes to make the barbecue sauce and cole slaw for almost 50 years.

Mom comes out of the kitchen to chat. She talks about her years at Allman's and how fortunate she is to be here. We're getting along famously, which makes me think I've softened her up, so I pop the question: How do you make the slaw taste so good?

She laughs. "I ain't telling you!" she says.

Dessert? Drive north on US 1 for a few blocks, turn right on Princess Anne Street, and look for Carl's—a frozen custard stand with a walk-up

The multi-use Mt. Vernon Trail connects George Washington's Mt. Vernon estate with Washington D.C.

The popular **Mt. Vernon Trail**, an 18-mile, multi-use paved path, hugs the Virginia shore of the Potomac River between Theodore Roosevelt Island, near the Lincoln Memorial, to Mt. Vernon. The trail goes through a marsh and public parks and past the end of the runway at Reagan National Airport. Mt. Vernon provides racks to park your bicycle, but be sure to bring along a serious bike lock. Old Town is in the middle of the trail, which is mostly flat, always scenic and a wonderful way to get a little exercise and get to Mt. Vernon. At a comfortable pace with occasional stops, you can pedal to Mt. Vernon from Old Town in less than 2 hours. Just know you likely won't be alone: roughly 1 million people use the trail annually, so you'll likely encounter walkers, joggers, bicyclists, young parents pushing babies in strollers, and, on weekdays, commuters. The trail is accessible to several Metro subway stops along the way, and you can park at a number of locations along the trail, including Mt. Vernon and Theodore Roosevelt Island, but spaces are limited, particularly on weekends.

window. Lines are often long because the homemade custard is so good, but don't be discouraged; they move fast, in part because the choices are only vanilla, chocolate, or strawberry. Just be ready to order when it's your turn. Like Allman's, it's an institution.

We drive north, past the turnoff for Mt. Vernon, which will be our destination for tomorrow. We have visited there before and discovered it's best to leave plenty of time to enjoy the museums, tour the house, and walk the grounds. Tonight we still stay in Old Town Alexandria, the one-time colonial seaport that is not exactly a "back roads" location, but it's lively and convenient and less than 10 miles north of Mt. Vernon. It will be an easy drive—or bicycle ride.

A historic district, Old Town has been a bustling place since Scottish merchants arrived in the 1740s. Today, the area is still known for its shopping, as well as its diverse restaurants and art galleries. Colonial homes and churches give the place a step-back-in-time charm. I like Old Town for all of those reasons and for this one: you can walk it.

We are staying at a Hampton Inn on King Street at the western edge of Old Town, about 16 blocks from the waterfront. It's a Friday night, and rates at many hotels here, like this one, offer reduced weekend rates. Free trolleys periodically run up and down the street, but we decide to walk. King Street is Old Town's primary thoroughfare, lined with trendy shops, antique stores, and booksellers, as well as bars and restaurants, with historical sites like Gadsby's Tavern and the Stabler-Leadbeater Apothecary Museum just a few steps away.

When hunger calls, Old Town is the place to be. I keep a running tab in my head of restaurants we walk past: Greek, Chinese, Italian, French, Moroccan, Thai, Mexican, Irish. You can't go wrong at venerable King Street eateries such as The Warehouse Bar & Grill or The Wharf, or at a place like the upscale Restaurant Eve, on South Pitt Street, operated by Cathal Armstrong, considered one of the top chefs in America. Alexandria itself has a reputation as an up-and-coming dining destination.

But on this night, we want something simple, and we want it at the waterfront, so we pick up dinner at the food court—we settle on Ethiopian and Chinese fare—adjacent to the Torpedo Factory Art Center, as the name suggests, a one-time torpedo factory that's been transformed into three stories of art studios and shops. After dinner, we wander through the art center, peeking in the studios to view the work of local artists.

For a holiday flavor, visit here the first weekend of December for the city's annual Scottish Christmas Walk Weekend, which features a Saturday morning parade that attracts thousands of spectators and dogs wearing kilts. In the evening, boats of all sizes sail up and down the Potomac, showing up off their holiday decorations. The illuminated boats make for quite a sight, with the U.S. Capitol in the distance. Make sure to pack an extra sweater; the waterfront can be chilly on a December evening.

In the morning, we head to George Washington's Mt. Vernon Estate & Gardens. Used to be you could stop by, walk through the house, and be on your way, but if you really want to see the place and learn about Washington you should plan to spend most of a day. You can still tour the house and see the study where he pondered and the bedroom where he died and uttered his last words, "'Tis well." Sit on George and Martha's back porch (or maybe it's the front porch) and admire the unparalleled view of the Potomac. Whatever you do, leave time for recent additions: the Ford Orientation Center and the Donald W. Reynolds Museum and Education Center, featuring 23 galleries and theaters and built largely underground so sheep can still graze on a pasture above it. To tell Washington's story, the education center draws on high-tech interactive exhibits such as the 4-D theater where "snow" falls while the general crosses the icy Delaware River on the screen. The museum relies on family artifacts to provide a sense of what life was like for the Washingtons. You can even visit Washington's

George Washington's Mt. Vernon Estate & Gardens sit on a bluff above the Potomac River. DEAN NORTON

distillery, which has been reconstructed and is in operation and open for tours.

A shrewd businessman and capable farmer, Washington built Mt. Vernon into an 8,000-acre estate that today has been reduced to 500 acres. Still, there is much to see and do just walking the grounds and gardens. For dining, I've eaten at both the perfectly fine food court and the sit-down Mt. Vernon Inn, where, I cannot tell a lie, I really enjoy a slice of cherry pie.

IN THE AREA

Accommodations

Hampton Inn Alexandria-Old Town, 1616 King Street, Alexandria. Call 703-299-9900. Within walking distance of Old Town historic sites and King Street Metro station. Web site: http://www.hamptoninn.com.

Stratford Hall, 483 Great House Road, Stratford. Call 804-493-8038. Two guest houses and guest cabins on the plantation. Web site: http://www.stratfordhall.org.

Attractions and Recreation

George Washington Birthplace National Monument, 1732 Popes Creek Road, Washington's Birthplace. Call 804-224-1732. Web site: http://www.nps.gov/gewa.

George Washington's Ferry Farm, 268 Kings Highway, Fredericksburg. Call 540-370-0732. Web site: http://www.ferryfarm.org.

George Washington's Mt. Vernon Estate and Gardens, 3200 Mt. Vernon Memorial Highway, Mt. Vernon. Call 703-780-2000. Web site: http://www.mountvernon.org.

Ingleside Vineyards, 5872 Leedstown Road, Oak Grove. Call 804-224-8687. Web site: http://www.inglesidevineyards.com.

Mt. Vernon Trail, George Washington Memorial Parkway Headquarters, Turkey Run Park, McLean. Call 703-289-2500. Web site: http://www.nps.gov/archive/gwmp/mvt.html.

Stratford Hall Plantation, 483 Great House Road, Stratford. Call 804-493-8038. Web site: http://www.stratfordhall.org.

Westmoreland State Park, 1650 State Park Road, Montross. Call 804-493-8821. Web site: http://www.dcr.virginia.gov/state_parks/wes.shtml.

White Oak Civil War Museum, 985 White Oak Road, Falmouth. Call 540-371-4234. Web site: http://www.whiteoakmuseum.com.

Dining

Allman's Bar-B-Q, 1299 Jeff Davis Highway, Fredericksburg. Call 540-373-9881. Web site: http://www.allmansbarbeque.com.

Carl's Frozen Custard, 2200 Princess Anne Street, Fredericksburg. Call 540-373-1776.

Restaurant Eve, 110 South Pitt Street, Alexandria. Call 703-706-0450. Elegant and, according to reviews, exceptional. Two dining choices: Chef's Tasting Room and The Bistro. Web site: http://www.restauranteve.com.

Riverboat on the Potomac, 301 Beach Terrace, Colonial Beach. Call 804-224-7055. Web site: http://www.theriverboat.net.

The Warehouse Bar & Grill, 214 King Street, Alexandria. Call 703-683-6868. Prime aged steaks, and seafood. Web site: http://www.warehouse barandgrill.com.

The Wharf, 119 King Street, Alexandria. Call 703-836-2836. Seafood. Web site: http://www.wharfrestaurant.com.

Other Contacts

Alexandria Visitor Center, 221 King Street, Alexandria. Call 703-746-3301. Web site: http://visitalexandriava.com.

Northern Neck Tourism Council, P.O. Box 1707, Warsaw. Call 1-800-393-6180. Web site: http://www.northernneck.org.

Fredericksburg Visitor Center, 706 Caroline Street, Fredericksburg. Call 540-373-1776. Web site: http://www.visitfred.com.

CHAPTER

9

From Stonewall to Madison

Manassas, Montpelier, and a drive through Virginia's horse country

Estimated length: 75 miles
Estimated time: Day trip.

Getting there: The visitor center for sprawling **Manassas National Battlefield Park** is at the intersection of US 29 and VA 234. From I-95, take Exit 152B and follow VA 234 north for about 24 miles to the park entrance, just past Northern Virginia Community College. From I-66, take Exit 47B and follow VA 234 north through one traffic light and past the community college.

Highlights: A little bit of everything representative of Virginia. Civil War history is on this route, primarily traveling US 29 and US 15, from **Manassas National Battlefield** to the town of **Gordonsville**: lovely scenery in the foothills, small towns, horse country, home of a U.S. president, bed-and-breakfast inns, and wineries.

LEFT: The Stonewall Jackson statue, near the visitor center, is a good place to start a tour of Manassas National Battlefield.

You can show up at Manassas National Battlefield Park any time you'd like, but get there, as I did, at dawn and stand at the larger-than-life statue of Confederate General Thomas J. "Stonewall" Jackson, bathed in day's first light. Crickets chirp and birds sing as dewdrops drip from the still cannons, and deer scamper across the deserted grounds. You don't have to be a Civil War buff to fast develop an appreciation for this place.

The visitor center, of course, is not open at dawn, but the property is ripe for strolling or jogging, which a lot of local residents seem to do. You can wait to follow a ranger around, or you can take a self-guided tour of this hallowed ground where thousands were killed and the stage was set— twice—for a brutal war of brother versus brother.

The battlefield, site of the first major land battle of the war and then a second one 13 months later, used to be on the back roads of the state. Now, it is a rare green space in the suburban sprawl of Northern Virginia. Preser-vationists and the National Park Service have fought to keep it so, fending off an interstate highway, a shopping mall, a housing development, and even a theme park. Still, the roads that crisscross the park are laden with traffic, particularly at rush hours when commuters are going to work or heading home. The occasional jet from nearby Dulles International Airport roars overhead.

Even so, this is a place of great significance and meaning, as your mind drifts back to what transpired here. You can almost hear the cannon fire and the blood-curdling Rebel yell. The first battle, also known as Bull Run for the stream that runs through the park, was fought on a hot Sunday in July 1861, attracting the curious from Washington to bring their picnic baskets and parasols and watch from nearby hillsides. This was supposed to be skir-mish at which Union troops would squelch the Southern uprising. Instead, it merely ignited the larger conflagration. The Confederates won this bat-tle and the second, but at a steep price for the nation: Nearly 4,000 troops were killed and more than 17,000 wounded at both. Scores went missing.

The park features an extensive system of trails, or you can drive to some of the far-flung sites of the 5,000-acre park. Let's get started. Walk the 1-mile Henry Hill Loop Trail, visit the rebuilt Henry House, and pause for a moment at the grave of Judith Carter Henry, the only civilian killed at First Manassas when artillery fire hit her house. Across US 29, visit the Stone House, which served as a field hospital in both battles. Less than a mile north on US 29, you'll find the famed Stone Bridge, with Bull Run trickling beneath it.

You won't want to miss Chinn Ridge, where both battles ended. Of course, at some point you should go by the visitor center, take a look at the artifacts and exhibits, and watch the fine orientation movie that captures the history of the place. There's an extensive bookstore, too.

Manassas is important to Virginians for another reason: this is where Jackson became "Stonewall." During First Manassas, Confederate General Barnard Bee, upon seeing Jackson and his men watching and waiting in the distance, is reported to have said, "There is Jackson standing like a stone wall."

The prevailing opinion is that Bee was being complimentary, likening his colleague to a sturdy fortress. But at least one soldier who heard the comment believed it was a snide remark, as in, "There stands Jackson doing nothing." We'll never know for certain, as Bee was killed in battle.

Head south on US 29 for less than 20 miles to Warrenton, the seat of lovely Fauquier County and the county's shopping and business hub. This is horse country. US 29 and US 15, which joined it before Warrenton) is a pretty drive, but you might consider venturing off in the countryside toward The Plains, a dozen miles north on US 17 and VA 245, which goes even deeper into the land of horse farms, and makes for a most pleasant expedition, motoring along tree-lined lanes, rolling green pastures, and long stretches of rail fences. If you venture as far as The Plains, you might check out the Great Meadow Events Center where you can catch an occasional steeplechase or regular polo match.

As you head south on US 15/29, Culpeper comes up in 25 miles. Another historic small town, Culpeper is a nice place for a stop, with museums, antique shops, and a variety of restaurants.

Another 20 miles south on US 15 (by this time, US 29 has veered off), as we go by bucolic scenes of pastureland and grazing cattle, brings us to the town of Orange. The town's visitor center is in the old rail station, a good place to stop for brochures and answers to travel questions about Central Virginia. Walk along Main Street and check out antique shops and art galleries. Dining options are not a problem here, either: from upscale Elmwood at Sparks to The Hornet's Nest, offering a more basic atmosphere with great barbecue and other familiar comfort foods.

Arranging a stay in this area is made easier by a partnership of area bed-and-breakfast inns—the Inns of Montpelier—that banded together after Montpelier, the home of President James Madison underwent a $24 million restoration and in the process became a major tourist attraction for

James Madison's Montpelier underwent a major restoration to return it to its 19th century form. KENNETH M. WYNER, COURTESY OF THE MONTPELIER FOUNDATION

the first time. The Inn at Westwood Farm, less than a mile from Montpelier, is among that group. Innkeepers Jay Billie and Elizabeth Goeke left the fast lane of life in suburban Washington D.C. to come to the solitude of Orange to transform the 1910 farmhouse into a bed-and-breakfast and busy themselves with welcoming guests, growing vegetables, and tending to a henhouse full of chickens laying dozens of eggs a day. Billie says he and Goeke and the other Inns at Montpelier innkeepers consider themselves "the concierges" of the entire area, not just for the particular establishments.

Ten minutes farther south and we find ourselves in Gordonsville, a small town with a surprising number of good places to eat, plus a Civil War museum. Before the war, the Exchange Hotel was a popular stop for travelers on the trains that came through town; during the war, it became a hospital where 70,000 troops—Confederate and Union—were treated. Now, it's a museum with—some say—ghosts.

For a small town, Gordonsville offers an intriguing mix of shopping possibilities, from antique shops to home décor stores. Known as the fried chicken capital of the world in the late 1800s, because of the townspeople who would greet train passengers with trays of chicken and other fare, Gordonsville remains a good place to stop for food. Toliver House, specializing in "simple elegance," and Pomme, offering a French menu that attracts diners from all around, are gourmet restaurants a block apart. In between, the Gordonsville Deli has homemade food and free WiFi.

For too long, James Madison, the fourth U.S. president, was often the most overlooked of America's Founding Fathers, in part, perhaps, because his home, **Montpelier**, wasn't open to the public. For more than 100 years, the 2,650-acre estate, off US 20 west of Orange, was in private hands and, unlike Washington's **Mt. Vernon** and Jefferson's **Monticello**, closed to the public. During that period, the home also had been transformed into something quite different than what James and Dolley Madison knew when they lived there: a 55-room mansion covered in pink stucco.

Montpelier was bequeathed to the National Trust for Historic Preservation in the 1980s and finally opened to the public. In the early years of the 21st century, the mansion underwent a five-year facelift—undoubtedly one of the great projects of historic preservation of our time—to return it to its configuration during Madison's time. The restoration, completed in 2008, included razing the wings added since the Madisons lived there, reducing the number of rooms from 55 to 26, and stripping off the stucco to reveal the original bare brick. One thing has remained constant through the years: the exquisite view of the Blue Ridge Mountains from the front porch.

Visitors can now tour the house, including the second-floor library where the shy, modest Madison—who drafted the Bill of Rights, authored The Federalist Papers, and is called the "the Father of the Constitution"—did his writing. When you go, you also must visit the modern visitor center, featuring a theater, gallery, and shop. Tour the formal garden and Madison's 200-acre Landmark Forest. Hands-on demonstrations of crafts and cooking take place outdoors in warm weather. Archaeological digs—and a search for original furnishings lost after Dolley Madison had to sell Montpelier in 1844 to pay off debts—are ongoing.

Madison may never catch Washington or Jefferson in public stature, historically speaking, but his home is catching up as a tourist attraction. Visitors have been flocking in record numbers to the home since it was restored, truly making Montpelier the newest old president's home in the land.

Wineries are sprinkled throughout this region, but one of the best, Barboursville Vineyards, is 6 miles west of Gordonsville on US 33. In a state that's rapidly gaining a national—and in some cases worldwide—reputation for fine wines, Barboursville is a premier destination. The winery's Palladio Restaurant, specializing in Northern Italian cuisine, has developed an equally impressive reputation for fine dining. You will be hard-pressed to find a better place to spend an afternoon or end a day's journey.

The old Exchange Hotel in Gordonsville, served as a hospital during the Civil War, and now houses a Civil War museum.

IN THE AREA

Accommodations

Inns at Montpelier, a partnership of bed-and-breakfast inns within 15 miles of Montpelier, James Madison's home, at Montpelier Station. Web site: http://www.innsatmontpelier.com.

Attractions and Recreation

Civil War Museum at the Exchange Hotel, 400 S. Main Street, Gordonsville. Call 540-832-2944. Former hotel and Civil War hospital. Web site: http://www.hgiexchange.org.

James Madison's Montpelier, 11407 Constitution Highway, Montpelier Station. Call 540-672-2728. Estate of fourth president of the United States. Web site: http://www.montpelier.org.

Manassas National Battlefield, 6511 Sudley Road, Manassas. Call 703-361-1339. Site of two major Civil War battles. Web site: http://www.nps.gov/mana.

Barboursville Vineyards, 17655 Winery Road, Barboursville. Call 540-832-3824. Winery at 18th-century estate, with Palladio Restaurant, featuring Northern Italian-inspired menu. Web site: http://www.barboursville wine.net.

Dining

Baby Jim's Snack Bar, 701 N. Main Street, Culpeper. Call 540-825-9212. A tiny, old-fashioned burger joint and Culpeper tradition, featuring hamburgers, hot dogs, fries, and milk shakes. Web site: http://www.chopped onion.com/id81.html.

Elmwood at Sparks, 124 W. Main Street, Orange. Call 540-672-0060. Innovative menu focusing on local ingredients, blending French and New American cuisine. Web site: http://www.elmwoodcatering.com.

It's About Thyme, 128 East Davis Street, Culpeper. Call 540-825-4264. European country cuisine, adjacent to Thyme Market, an upscale deli, in Culpeper's historic district. Web site: http://www.thymeinfo.com.

Restaurant Pomme, 115 S. Main Street, Gordonsville. Call 540-832-0130. French cuisine. Web site: http://www.restaurantpomme.com.

Toliver House Restaurant, 209 N. Main Street, Gordonsville. Call 540-832-0000. Fine dining and comfort food on a wide-ranging menu, plus Nathaniel Gordon Pub. Web site: http://www.toliverhouse.com.

Other Contacts

Fauquier County Tourism, 35 Culpeper Street, Warrenton. Call 540-349-1231. Web site: http://www.visitfauquier.com.

Town of Culpeper Tourism, 111 S. Commerce Street, Culpeper. Call 540-727-0611. Web site: http://www.visitculpeperva.com.

Thomas Jefferson's Monticello, reflecting in the fish pond, is an architectural masterpiece. THOMAS JEFFERSON FOUNDATION / MARY PORTER

CHAPTER

10

Mr. Jefferson's Neighborhod

In and around Charlottesville, you'll find history, wine, and good pizza, too

Estimated length: 75 miles
Estimated time: Weekend

Getting there: To reach Monticello, take I-64 to Charlottesville Exit 121 (from the east) or Exit 121A from the west. Take VA 20 South to second stoplight, and turn left onto VA 53 (Thomas Jefferson Parkway). Follow VA 53 East for just less than 2 miles. Immediately after passing under the stone-arch Saunders Bridge, exit right onto the roadway that leads over the bridge and onto the grounds of Monticello.

Highlights: Thomas Jefferson's **Monticello** and James Monroe's **Ash Lawn**. Before you come down the mountain, apple- or peach-picking (or whatever they have fresh) at **Carter's Mountain Orchard**. A visit to the lively **Downtown Mall** and a drive through the **University of Virginia**. The **Monticello Wine Trail**. A pie at **Crozet Pizza** and bagels at **Bodo's**. Just motoring around the lovely countryside in the foothills of the **Blue Ridge Mountains**.

If you're playing the License Plate Game, there's no better place to start than the parking lot at Monticello on a summer morning. We count no fewer than 25 different states represented in the lot, and that's just what we happened to see on our way to the visitor center. Thomas Jefferson's still got it. Going on 200 years after his death, the third U.S. president remains the big attraction in Charlottesville—his home, his university, his name on roads, churches, and vineyards—so it only makes sense you ought to begin any driving tour of Charlottesville at Monticello. Besides, it's an architectural masterpiece, and a place into which Jefferson poured his heart, soul, and much of his money for almost 60 years to make it just right.

A trip to Monticello begins at the Thomas Jefferson Visitor Center and Smith Education Center, five pavilions around a central courtyard offering learning, dining, and shopping before you ever get to the house itself. You acquire your tour tickets here, with a designated time for going in the house. It's not a terribly long walk up the hill to the house, we are told, but it is uphill and on a warm day you can be drenched in a hurry. So, we elect to take the shuttle bus to the mansion and walk back—downhill—after our tour.

Speaking of walks, we didn't have time on this trip, but the Saunders-Monticello Trail is a nice option. It stretches from a parking lot near the intersection of VA 20 and VA 5 for 2 miles up the mountain to Monticello. The grade is gentle, the footing is good, and the views of the surrounding mountains are something you can't get from the road.

Once at the top of the mountain, we stroll along the 1,000-foot-long garden plateau where Jefferson cultivated more than 300 kinds of vegetables, in addition to fruits and flowers. We are told the garden looks much the same as it did in Jefferson's day. Jefferson dabbled in gardening, weather, design, just about everything. He was a most interesting and interested man.

We walk around the small fishpond where Jefferson kept fish for eating and into which a classmate of mine stumbled during a school field trip many years ago. Funny, that's the one thing I remember from that visit. This time, no one in my party gets wet. When the time arrives for our tour, we enter the house and hear how there was a time, after Jefferson's death, when hay was stored in this jewel of a home and how the Levy family saved it from ruin. We marvel at Jefferson's little touches: the great clock in the entry hall, the dumbwaiter, his writing desk. The place is magnificent.

We walk down the hill, past Jefferson's grave, back to the visitor center to watch a movie that brings Jefferson's life into focus, and to eat lunch at the Café at Monticello, where you can buy sandwiches, salads, and baked goods. After lunch, we head 2 miles farther east on VA 53 to Jefferson's neighbor's house: President James Monroe's Ash Lawn-Highland, a modest home that stands in stark contrast to Monticello's splendor. Monroe's original house was so small, our tour guide tells us, overnight guests might have been offered a blanket to sleep on the floor next to Monroe's canopy bed. In all, Monticello covers 5,000 acres; Ash Lawn-Highland 535. Their homes are reflections of the men: Jefferson was bold, intellectual, and famous; Monroe, the fifth U.S. president, unassuming, deliberative, and compared to some presidents, relatively unfamiliar to many Americans. But Monroe led a distinguished life of public service, crossing the frigid Delaware River as an 18-year-old soldier with George Washington and later negotiating the Louisiana Purchase on behalf of Jefferson's administration.

Said Jefferson, "Monroe was so honest that if you turned his soul inside out there would not be a spot on it."

We leave Monroe's home, driving down a long lane lined with ash trees. Before coming down from the mountain, you might want to stop at Michie Tavern, which has been accommodating travelers with food and drink since 1784. Or you might, as we do, stop at Carter Mountain Orchard, steer your vehicle up the steep gravel drive, and see what's growing. We usually make an annual autumn trek to the orchard, a family-run, pick-your-own sort of place, to pluck apples from their trees, eat apple doughnuts, and drink hot apple cider on a chilled afternoon. Maybe buy a pumpkin, too. We're too early for apples or pumpkins on this trip, but we find baskets of freshly picked peaches—and peach doughnuts. We buy a bag of peaches and a bag of doughnuts. They do not last long.

At the foot of the Blue Ridge, Charlottesville is a city of 40,000 with a small-town feel and much to offer. You can pretty much go in any direction and find something fun to do. Spend some time on the Downtown Mall, on Main Street, one of those bricked-over pedestrian developments that actually attracts people. The mall also has 120 stores, 30 restaurants, and a pavilion at the east end that's a community gathering spot, with concerts on Friday evenings and other well-attended shows through the year. We show up on a Saturday afternoon, and the mall is jumping. It's nice to see a downtown area alive with activity. People dine at outdoor cafes, and browse clothing shops, art galleries, and used bookstores. We join in before heading out of town for more rural destinations.

Stay on University Avenue, which is also US 250-Business, heading west out of town, where it becomes Ivy Road. About 2 miles outside of town you

James Monroe's Ash Lawn is a study in modesty compared to neighbor Jefferson's home.

On the way into the country, though, take Main Street west, veering to the right onto University Avenue. This will take you to the **University of Virginia**, where, it's important to remember, you should never refer to *The Grounds* as a "campus." Park (if you can find a spot) and roam **The Corner**, a stretch of restaurants and shops, roughly from 12½ Street to Madison Lane, central to life at UVa for students, faculty, and staff. Eat a sandwich at **Littlejohn's New York Delicatessen**. Buy a UVa T-shirt at **Mincer's**. Then walk past Madison Lane for a good look at The Rotunda, designed by Jefferson to be the architectural and academic heart of the university. He appears to have succeeded. Tours are available.

pass the Boar's Head Inn, a resort offering first-class dining, lodging, and golf. We have something a little more basic in mind, so we keep going west for another 10 miles, staying straight on VA 240 when US 250 bends to the left. We come to Crozet and, more specifically, Crozet Pizza, a small institution with a big reputation. The pizzas coming from the kitchen have gained fame and followers far and wide. Homemade dough and the right combination of sauce and spices apparently make the difference with the hand-tossed pizzas. My 15-year-old daughter and I are eager to see what the fuss is about. We conduct our research in a window booth of the cozy shop with a wood stove and a screen door that gently slaps closed every time another customer comes or goes. We share a large pie. The verdict: It's as good as we've ever had.

The farms and foothills make this such a pretty part of Virginia. If you're interested in fresh produce, pay a visit to Chiles Peach Orchard, a nearby farm market with peaches and other locally grown fruits and vegetables, May through Thanksgiving. To get there from Crozet Pizza, we go to the intersection with Crozet Avenue, turn left, go under the railroad bridge and then make a quick right onto Jarman's Gap Road, drive for 2.5 miles and make a slight left onto Greenwood Road.

Or go right at Crozet Avenue and head up VA 240, which eventually will bring you to White Hall and White Hall Vineyards, part of the Monticello Wine Trail. To get to White Hall Vineyards from White Hall on VA 240, take VA 810 north to Break Heart Road, which becomes Sugar Ridge Road. The winery is 1.5 miles ahead on your right.

If you want to walk off the pizza, stop by Ivy Creek Natural Area, a 215-acre preserve just north of Charlottesville that's a refuge for wildlife and

MONTICELLO WINE TRAIL

Thomas Jefferson was a wine connoisseur but a frustrated vintner. He had no luck growing grapes, but his vision of Virginia as home to a robust wine industry has come, so to speak, to fruition. His region of the state has been particularly successful, and the **Monticello Wine Trail**, consisting of nearly two dozen wineries within a half-hour drive of Charlottesville, is testament to that. Included in the group: **Jefferson Vineyards**, in the shadow of Monticello. Many offer tastings and tours. Some have restaurants.

Afton Mountain Vineyards, 234 Vineyard Lane, Afton. Call 540-456-8667. Web site: http://www.aftonmountainvineyards.com.

Barboursville Vineyards, intersection of VA 33 and VA 20, Barboursville. Call 540-832-3824. Web site: http://www.barboursvillewine.com.

Blenheim Vineyards, 31 Blenheim Farm, Charlottesville. Call 434-293-5366. Web site: http://www.blenheimvineyards.com.

Burnley Vineyards, 4500 Winery Lane, Barboursville. Call 540-832-2828. Web site: http://www.burnleywines.com.

Cardinal Point Vineyard & Winery, 9423 Batesville Road, Afton. Call 540-456-8400. Web site: http://www.cardinalpointwinery.com.

First Colony Winery, 1650 Harris Creek Road, Charlottesville. Call 434-979-7105. Web site: http://www.firstcolonywinery.com.

Flying Fox Vineyard, 27 Chapel Hollow Road, Afton. Call 434-361-1692. Web site: http://www.flyingfoxvineyard.com.

Horton Vineyards, 6399 Spotswood Trail, Gordonsville. Call 540-832-7440. Web site: http://www.hvwine.com.

Jefferson Vineyards, 1353 Thomas Jefferson Parkway, Charlottesville. Call 434-977-3042. Web site: http://www.jeffersonvineyards.com.

Keswick Vineyards, 1575 Keswick Winery Drive, Keswick. Call 434-244-3341. Web site: http://www.keswickvineyards.com.

King Family Vineyards, 6550 Roseland Farm, Crozet. Call 434-823-7800. Web site: http://www.kingfamilyvineyards.com.

Kluge Estate Winery, 100 Grand Cru Drive, Charlottesville. Call 434-977-3895. Web site: http://www.klugeestate.com.

Lovingston Winery, 885 Freshwater Cove Lane, Lovingston. Call 434-263-8467. Web site: http://www.lovingstonwinery.com.

The area around Charlottesville is rich in vineyards and wineries, like Jefferson Vineyards, just down the mountain from Monticello.

Mountfair Vineyards, 4875 Fox Mountain Road, Crozet. Call 434-823-7605. Web site: http://www.mountfair.com.

Pollak Vineyards, 330 Newtown Road, Greenwood. Call 540-456-8844. Web site: http://www.pollakvineyards.com" \t "_blank.

Prince Michel Vineyards and Winery, 154 Winery Lane, Leon. Call 1-800-800-9463. Web site: http://www.princemichel.com.

Stone Mountain Vineyards, 1376 Wyatt Mountain Road, Dyke. Call 434-990-9463. Web site: http://www.stonemountainvineyards.com.

Sugarleaf Vineyards, 3613 Walnut Branch Lane, North Garden. Call 434-984-4272. Web site: http://www.sugarleafvineyards.com.

Sweely Estate Winery, 6109 Wolftown-Hood Road, Madison. Call 540-948-9005. Web site: http://www.sweelyestatewinery.com.

Veritas Vineyard & Winery, 145 Saddleback Farm, Afton. Call 540-456-8000. Web site: http://www.veritaswines.com.

White Hall Vineyards, 5282 Sugar Ridge Road, White Hall. Call 434-823-8615. Web site: http://www.whitehallvineyards.com.

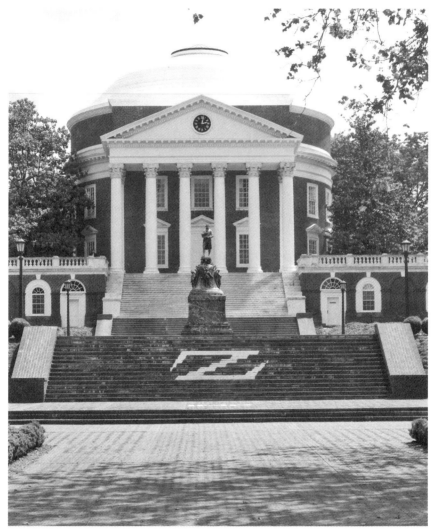

Designed by Jefferson, the Rotunda is the focal point of the grounds of the University of Virginia.

wildflowers, and a sanctuary for people wanting a quiet retreat. It's on Earlysville Road, just off Hydraulic Road, a little west of US 29. You can hear your own footsteps as you walk the 7 miles of wooded trails. The park is on the site of an old farm once owned by a freed slave who used money earned through sharecropping to purchase the property. Local residents partnered with The Nature Conservancy to buy the farm when development seemed imminent. Enjoy it, but follow the rules: no bikes, no jogging, no picnics.

We make one more stop before leaving town: Bodo's Bagels, a locally popular chain that is said to be one of the things people say they miss most when they move from Charlottesville. Bodo's is said to produce "authentic New York water" bagels all day. We visit the location on US 29, also known as Emmet Street, just south of the US 250 bypass. We pick up a dozen fresh bagels. The bag is warm. No doubt, Mr. Jefferson would be pleased.

IN THE AREA

Accommodations

Boars Head Inn, 200 Ednam Drive, Charlottesville. Call 434-296-2181. Resort with lodging, fine dining, golf, spa, hiking, tennis on a 573-acre estate. Web site: http://www.boarsheadinn.com.

Clifton Inn, 1296 Clifton Inn Drive, Charlottesville. Call 434-971-1800. The property was once part of a land grant belonging to Thomas Jefferson's father, Peter. Now a luxury hotel with 18 rooms and a restaurant. Web site: http://www.cliftoninn.net.

Hilton Garden Inn, 1793 Richmond Road, Charlottesville. Call 434-979-4442. One of the newest hotels in the Charlottesville area. Web site: http://www.charlottesville.stayhgi.com.

Inn at Court Square, 410 E. Jefferson Street, Charlottesville. Call 434-295-2800. Guest rooms with working fireplaces and private baths, steps from the historic Court Square district where Thomas Jefferson, James Madison, and James Monroe practiced law in a courthouse still in use today. Web site: http://www.innatcourtsquare.com.

Attractions and Recreation

Ash Lawn-Highland, 1000 James Monroe Parkway, Charlottesville. Call 434-293-8000. Web site: http://www.ashlawnhighland.org.

Carter Mountain Orchard, 1435 Carters Mountain Trail, Charlottesville. Call 434-977-1833. Web site: http://www.cartermountainorchard.com.

Chiles Peach Orchard, 1351 Greenwood Road, Crozet. Call 434-823-1583. Web site: http://www.chilespeachorchard.com.

Ivy Creek Natural Area, 1776 Earlysville Road, Charlottesville. Call 434-973-7772. Web site: http://www.ivycreekfoundation.org.

Michie Tavern, 683 Thomas Jefferson Parkway, Charlottesville. Call 434-977-1234. Web site: http://www.michietavern.com.

The Rotunda at the University of Virginia, University Avenue. Call 434-924-7969. Web site: http://www.virginia.edu/uvatours/rotunda.

Thomas Jefferson's Monticello, 931 Thomas Jefferson Parkway, Charlottesville. Call 434-984-9822. Web site: http://www.monticello.org.

Dining

Bodo's Bagels, 1418 Emmet Street, Charlottesville. Bagles made from scratch round-the-clock, plus sandwiches and salads. Web site: http://www.bodosbagels.com.

Crozet Pizza, 5794 Three Notch'd Road, Crozet. Call 434-823-2132. Family-operated pizza shop. Web site: http://www.crozetpizza.net.

Duner's, 4372 Ivy Road, Ivy. Call 434-293-8352. Casual fine dining 5 miles west of Charlottesville. Menu changes daily. Web site: http://www.dunersrestaurant.com.

Hamilton's Restaurant, 101 W. Main Street, Charlottesville. Call 434-295-6649. Contemporary American cuisine and award-winning wine list. Web site: http://www.hamiltonrestaurant.com.

Littlejohn's New York Delicatessen, 1427 University Avenue, Charlottesville. Subs, sandwiches, long hours, on The Corner. Call 434-977-0588.

The Local, 824 Hinton Avenue, Charlottesville. Call 434-984-9749. In the historic neighborhood of Belmont, The Local specializes in local food and beverages from the Charlottesville region. Its popularity makes reservations a must. Web site: http://www.thelocal-cville.com.

Other Contacts

Charlottesville Albemarle Convention & Visitor Bureau, 610 E. Main Street, Charlottesville. Call 434-293-6789. The bureau sells the President's Pass, a combination discounted ticket for touring Monticello, Ash Lawn-Highland, and Michie Tavern. Web site: http://www.pursuecharlottes ville.com.

Monticello Wine Trail. Web site: http://www.monticellowinetrail.com.

Lee surrendered to Grant at Appomattox Court House, still a bucolic setting in rural Central Virginia.

CHAPTER

11

Road to Appomattox

Follow Lee and Grant to the place where a fractured nation began to heal

Estimated length: 100 miles
Estimated time: A day-trip or two

Getting there: Take I-95 south of Richmond to Exit 61A, go east on VA 10, then 8 miles to Hopewell. Or south on I-295 from Richmond to Exit 15A, then east on VA 10 for 4 miles to Hopewell. Or north on I-295 to Exit 9A, then east on VA 36 for 2 miles to Hopewell.

Highlights: Civil War-related sites including General Ulysses S. Grant's headquarters at City Point in Hopewell, Petersburg National Battlefield, Pamplin Historical Park & The National Museum of the Civil War Soldier, and, of course, Appomattox Court House National Historical Park, where you can stand in the parlor of the reconstructed home where General Robert E. Lee surrendered to Grant. Along the way, tour a well-preserved 18th-century mansion, Weston Manor, in Hopewell, grab a chili dog at the Hopewell Quick Lunch, and browse the furniture stores of Farmville. If you bring your bicycle, you can pedal High Bridge Trail.

I divide my journey into two day-trips. You might want to spend a night or even make it a weekend as there's plenty enough to see here to support a longer trip. If you choose to spread the trip over two days, you might consider starting, as I did, in Hopewell, a sometimes overlooked city rich in history and friendly people.

Hopewell sits at the point where the Appomattox River flows into the James River, a logistically favorable location that, during the siege of nearby Petersburg, attracted Grant to set up his headquarters at Appomattox Plantation on a high bluff overlooking the spot where the two rivers come together. City Point, as this area is known, was one of the busiest seaports in the world during that period, serving as the supply center for 100,000 Union soldiers. President Lincoln sailed here in March 1865 aboard a steamboat, *River Queen,* to meet with Grant and plot the end of the war.

Come to City Point and feel the breeze blowing off the rivers. Visit the plantation, now called Appomattox Manor and a part of the Petersburg National Battlefield, and tour the mansion that was in near ruins after the war but has since been restored. Walk the grounds and peek in the modest log cabin Grant used as his headquarters. It hasn't been here all along. After the war, it was presented as a gift to Philadelphia, where it was a tourist attraction but eventually suffered from neglect and vandalism, falling into disrepair. After the National Park Service purchased Appomattox Manor in 1979, it returned Grant's cabin to City Point and restored it.

However, Hopewell is more than just the Civil War. The English colonists, who in May 1607 settled at Jamestown, 50 miles to the east, ventured up the James and considered the City Point area as a settlement location, but found the harbor too shallow and the Native Americans living here too dangerous. But the colonists came back soon enough. City Point was officially founded in 1613, meaning it is now the oldest continuously occupied settlement in the United States, according to *Old City Point and Hopewell,* a locally published history. (City Point was annexed in the 1920s by the city of Hopewell, which had developed around a DuPont factory just a few years earlier.) City Point grew into a shipping port for tobacco as plantations sprouted along the James and Appomattox Rivers. Construction on Appomattox Manor began in 1763; another nearby plantation home, Weston Manor, was built in 1769.

I drop by Weston, a Georgian mansion restored and now owned by the Historic Hopewell Foundation that's a couple of miles upriver from Appomattox Manor. Mary Mitchell Calos and Charlotte "Cholly" Easterling, longtime volunteers with the foundation and tireless community boosters, show me around. Weston is in remarkable shape. The oldest bricks in the foundation arrived as ballast in British ships in the 1700s. Much of the interior—including windows, most of the heart-pine flooring, and a substantial percentage of the moldings, wainscotings, chair rails—is

Grant's headquarters at City Point, now a part of Hopewell, sits on a bluff above where the Appomattox and James rivers converge.

original. The furnishings are not original, but many of the period antique pieces were donated by local residents, pointing up the community pride in this place.

And the stories are great. Calos and Easterling tell me about an incident in 1970 when work crews were restoring the house. Amid the hammering, someone heard something rolling around in the ceiling above the first floor. Pretty soon, a cannon ball fell through the ceiling. A bomb squad was called and needed to detonate the Civil War cannon ball, which the hammering apparently dislodged from its resting place of more than 100 years. The cannon ball, the figuring goes, came from federal gunboats on the river firing at Confederate cavalry in the area.

The main site, or Eastern Front, of Petersburg National Battlefield is less than 15 miles west of Hopewell. Take VA 36 west from Hopewell to I-295 and head south to Exit 3B and then west on US 460 to the entrance. The park actually includes 13 separate sites with three visitor centers along a 33-mile route. The Eastern Front visitor center tells the story of the siege of Petersburg and is the best place to go if you have time for only one stop. But if you have a full day to drive the entire route, which includes the Western Front at Five Forks where a dramatic Union victory ensured the collapse of Petersburg and Richmond, you'll be glad you did.

At lunchtime, Hopewell has a surprising variety of options, including Italian, Chinese, Mexican, Latin American, and, of course, barbecue. But I choose an old-time local favorite: **Hopewell Quick Lunch**, a small brick diner that's been serving the best chili dogs in town since 1927. I ask for cole slaw on mine, too. The beauty of the place, besides the secret chili recipe, the other stick-to-your-ribs fare, and the speed with which your meal is served, lies in the diversity and generations-long loyalty of its customers.

"Any day at the Quick Lunch you might see construction workers with muddy boots sitting next to men in business suits and ties," says my friend Pete Calos, Mary's husband, and a longtime customer of the Quick Lunch.

Mary Sue Krout grew up in Hopewell and has been a customer since 1966. She bought the place in 2008 and says the best part of the job is "I get to see old friends for breakfast and lunch every day."

At lunchtime, the place is usually hopping, with its tables, booths, and stools at the counter filled. Here's a tip: "When it's really busy you better not make eye contact with anyone standing up," Krout says with a laugh, "because they're waiting for your seat."

We like to take our bikes to the main site and ride along the paved tour road and, on occasion, on the off-road trails that twist and turn through the woods. The pedaling is easy and a great way to see the park. Don't miss the site of the Battle of the Crater, a July 1864 clash that began with Union soldiers constructing a 500-foot-long tunnel under the Confederate line. Union troops set off an explosion beneath the Confederates, instantly killing scores of Southern troops and creating a ghastly crater 30 feet deep. However, the battle proved to be a disaster for Union troops, many of whom advanced into the crater and to their deaths as the Confederates recovered and counter-attacked. More than 6,000 soldiers died in the battle, most of them Union troops. At the site, you can peer into a reconstruction of the tunnel.

Aside from the national park sites, you really should save some time for the stunningly good Pamplin Historical Park & The National Museum of the Civil War Soldier, a private and innovative park, 9 miles west of the Eastern Front site on US 460. Dr. Robert B. Pamplin Jr., a businessman and philanthropist in Portland, Oregon, whose family owned land in this area in the 1800s, purchased the property in the early 1990s to preserve a line of well-preserved earthworks constructed by Confederate troops. Grant's army overran the Confederate line on April 2, 1865, leading to the end of the siege of Petersburg and setting the stage for Lee's surrender at Appomattox a week later. The land-preservation effort turned into something much more when Pamplin set up an interpretative center and made plans to construct a more elaborate attraction. The park features four museums, four antebellum homes, and the National Museum of the Civil War Soldier, a high-tech, hands-on exhibition that tells the story of the common soldiers who fought the war.

I once spent the night at Pamplin as part of its Civil War Adventure Camp program, in which participants dress, march, eat, and sleep like Civil War soldiers. The uniform was scratchy, the marching a bit tiring, and the hardtack was, uh, hard. But the stew, cooked over an open fire, was mighty tasty. It was a great night.

Visitors can peer into the entrance of a re-creation of the Union tunnel at Petersburg National Battlefield.

For the second leg of our trip, we head to Appomattox Court House. You can retrace Lee's steps by following Virginia's Retreat, an official tourism trail of 25 stops with audio and visual interpretation at each site. The suggested time to devote to that trail alone is two days. Having the interest but not the time on this jaunt, we opt to drive US 460—the most direct route to Appomattox Court House, roughly 90 miles from Petersburg.

US 460 becomes the backroads equivalent of an interstate highway—four lanes with a grassy median in between—particularly west of Farmville. You get the feeling, though, much of the area along the route hasn't changed much in the days since Lee headed west from Petersburg with Grant in pursuit. Except for occasional small towns, farmland and thick woods dominate the landscape.

You might consider a stop at Farmville, an old tobacco market town on US 460, about 70 miles west of Petersburg. It's the home of **Longwood College**, and **Hampden-Sydney College** is just outside town. Farmville, a town of 7,000, also attracts lots of visitors shopping for furniture. **Green Front Furniture** fills 12 warehouses, wall to wall and floor to ceiling, with furniture, rugs, and all sorts of furnishings—including statues and other decorative garden art—at discount prices.

We stop for dinner at **Charley's Waterfront Café**, housed in a historic tobacco warehouse, overlooking the Appomattox River. One of the Green Front warehouses is next door. Family friendly, Charley's offers seafood, steaks, and pasta, as well as soups and sandwiches. My Cajun chicken alfredo was quite good.

Did someone say, "Exercise?" **The High Bridge Trail State Park,** a 34-mile, rails-to-trails, multi-use path for hiking, biking and horseback riding, comes through downtown Farmville. The trail's namesake, High Bridge, nearly a half-mile long, soars 160 feet above the Appomattox. The trail is being converted in stages, and 22 of the 34 miles were open as of spring 2010.

Well off the beaten path, Appomattox Court House National Historical Park probably has never received the widespread attention or appreciation it deserves. Tucked in the countryside of south-central Virginia, the understated park gives the appearance of a bucolic little village, which it was, but little hint of the momentous event that occurred here when Lee ended his desperate dash for supplies and reinforcements and decided discretion was indeed the better part of valor. The restored village, 2 miles northeast of the town of Appomattox on VA 24, looks very much as it did in 1865, when Lee and Grant met here.

We arrive in early afternoon and begin our look around at the visitor center, which is the reconstructed courthouse. The original burned to the ground in 1892. The visitor center provides context and perspective through artwork and artifacts, including the tabletop on which the terms of surrender were signed and the white towel that was the Confederates' first flag of truce. We stand on the porch of the original Clover Hill Tavern, a popular spot in those days because of its location on the Richmond-to-Lynchburg stagecoach road. In an extensive and detailed monologue, a costumed interpreter tells us about life in the village in the 1860s.

We walk over to the McLean House, the reconstructed home where

A living history interpreter describes 19th-century life at Clover Hill Tavern for visitors at Appomattox Court House National Historical Park.

the surrender took place April 9, 1865. The original house was dismantled in 1893 with plans to rebuild it elsewhere as a tourist attraction. The idea never came to fruition, and many of the original building materials were lost to damage and decay. Using detailed specifications and archaeological evidence, the National Park Service reconstructed the house on the original foundation. We stand in the parlor where Lee and Grant quite possibly saved a nation, adversaries who ended a most uncivil war in a most civil manner. Grant offered generous terms of surrender, Lee accepted, and the nation moved on. The house, by the way, was owned by Wilmer McLean, a businessman who earlier owned a home at Manassas: site of the first major land battle of the war four years earlier.

My favorite story from our tour was this: On the stage road, three days after the surrender, Grant assigned General Joshua Chamberlain to accept the formal surrender of arms from Lee's soldiers. As the ragged Confederate troops trudged into the village to lay down their weapons, Chamberlain called his men to attention and had them salute the Confederates as they approached. No cheers or taunts, just simple honor, respect, and dignity.

IN THE AREA

Accommodations

Babcock House Bed and Breakfast Inn, 250 Oakleigh Avenue, Appomattox. Call 434-352-9743. Set in an 1800s Victorian house, serving breakfast, lunch, and dinner. Web site: http://www.babcockhouse.com.

Longwood University Bed and Breakfast, 608 High Street, Farmville. Call 434-395-2617. A short walk to Longwood University and the shops of the town's historic district. Web site: http://www.babcockhouse.com.

Attractions and Recreation

Appomattox Court House National Historical Park, VA 24, Appomattox. Call 434-352-8987. Web site: http://www.nps.gov/apco.

Green Front Furniture, 316 N. Main Street, Farmville. Call 434-392-5943. A dozen warehouses of furniture and furnishings. Web site: http://www.greenfront.com.

High Bridge Trail State Park, 6888 Green Bay Road, Green Bay. (Park office.) Call 434-315-0457. Biking and hiking trail that runs through Farmville. Web site: http://www.dcr.virginia.gov/state_parks/hig.shtml.

Pamplin Historical Park and The National Museum of the Civil War Soldier, 6125 Boydton Plank Road, Petersburg. Call 804-861-2408. Web site: http://www.pamplinpark.org.

Petersburg National Battlefield, 1539 Hickory Hill Road, Petersburg. Call 804-732-3531. Web site: http://www.nps.gov/pete.

Weston Manor, 400 Weston Lane, Hopewell. Call 804-458-4682. Restored 18th-century home. Web site: http://www.historichopewell.org.

Dining

Baine's Books and Coffee, 20 Main Street, Appomattox. Call 434-352-3711. Panini sandwiches, soups, stews, lasagna, and, of course, coffee and

baked goods with live music on weekends. Web site: http://www.baines
books.com.

Charley's Waterfront Café, 201-B Mill Street, Farmville. Call 434-392-
1566. Lunch and dinner overlooking the Appomattox River. Web site:
http://www.charleyswaterfront.com.

Hopewell Quick Lunch, 113 Hopewell Street, Hopewell. Call 804-458-
6526. Diner serving breakfast and lunch.

Longstreet's Deli, 302 N Sycamore Street, Petersburg. Call 804 722-4372.
Sandwiches, specialty wines, and beers.

Luna International Restaurant, 208 E. Cawson Street, Hopewell. Call
804-452-5135. Latin American cuisine, featuring dishes from Bolivia,
Cuba, Mexico, Peru, and Spain in an atmosphere of casual fine dining.
Web site: http://www.lunaexpress.com. Sister restaurant in Petersburg's
Old Towne section: **Andrade's International Restaurant,** 7 Bollingbrook
Street Call 804-733-1515. Web site: http://www.andradesinternational
.com.

The Corner Grill, 115 N. Church Street, Appomattox. Call 434-352-3196.
Country cooking.

Other Contacts

Appomattox Visitor Information. 214 Main Street, Appomattox. Call
434-352-8999. Web site: http://www.tourappomattox.com.

City of Hopewell. Web site: http://www.hopewellva.gov.

Civil War Traveler. Web site: http://www.civilwartraveler.com.

Old Towne Petersburg. Restored historic district featuring restaurants
and antique shops. Web site: http://www.oldtownepetersburg.com.

Virginia's Retreat, 425 Cockade Alley, Petersburg. Driving tour of Lee's
Retreat. Web site: http://www.varetreat.com.

The one-lane Meems Bottom Bridge near Mt. Jackson is a step back in time.

12

The Valley Pike

An excursion on US 11 yields beauty, fun, and a bag of chips

Estimated length: 130 miles
Estimated time: 2 days

Getting there: This drive along US 11 stretches between **Winchester** to the north and Natural Bridge to the south. Winchester is just off I-81, about 15 miles south of the West Virginia line. **Natural Bridge** is just south of Lexington, near the intersection of I-64 and I-81. US 11, easily accessible in each of those cities, parallels I-81 through the **Shenandoah Valley**.

Highlights: Uncoiling through fertile farmland, US 11 stitches together a series of splendid towns and cities such as **Lexington, Staunton, Harrisonburg, New Market, Woodstock,** and **Strasburg.** Lovely scenery dominates the drive. You will find Civil War history along the way and a number of venerable colleges and universities worth visiting even if they're not your alma mater, such as Lexington neighbors **Virginia Military Institute** and **Washington and Lee University.** You can drive over a natural wonder like **Natural Bridge** and walk around nearby **Foamhenge,** which is funny and clever, though not particularly natural. Besides Foamhenge, surprises include the **American Shakespeare Center** in Staunton, the **Route 11 Potato Chips** factory near Mt. Jackson, and the **Green Valley Book Fair,** where you can browse among the stacks of a half-million discount-priced books. If there's time, you can ski at **Massanutten Ski Resort** in **McGaheysville,** or tour one of the numerous caverns—**Endless**, **Luray**, or **Shenandoah**, among others.

Following the path of an old trail favored by Native Americans long before the English and other immigrants arrived, US 11 runs down the mountainous spine of Virginia for more than 300 miles, from Winchester in the north to Bristol in the south. (In all, US 11 extends from upper New York to Louisiana, one of the nation's old, great roadways.) In Virginia, it offers the fetching scenery of valley farmland and small-town America, a world away from interstate highway travel—but in reality usually only a mile or less from I-81, which replaced it beginning in the 1960s as the primary artery through the valley of Virginia. In fact, the interstate is sometimes visible from US 11, and on several occasions the old road crisscrosses the newer highway.

In the 1700s, pioneers and traders poured into the valley, using this route as a thoroughfare to a new life or to the next state. It became known as The Great Wagon Road. In the early 1800s, the commonwealth of Virginia partnered with a private firm to develop a large section of the trail into an actual road with tolls. In effect, the Valley Turnpike was one of the nation's first highways. During the Civil War, it served as an avenue for troop and artillery movement. The history runs deep.

The tolls are gone, and most of the traffic today is local, those merely passing through speed past on I-81, not knowing what they're missing. You can certainly drive US 11 from border to border, Winchester to Bristol, but for the purposes of this chapter I will travel between Lexington and Winchester. If you try to follow US 11 farther south, be aware that US 11 and I-81 merge as one at times, and have a good map handy if you try to follow the road through Roanoke.

Let's start at Winchester, a city of 25,000, home of the Shenandoah Apple Blossom Festival every April, and worthy of exploration. We stop for a stroll at the pedestrian mall in Old Town Winchester, among outdoor cafes and numerous shops. With sufficient time, you might consider a walking tour of the city's historic district to admire the architecture and to drop by one of the numerous museums, such as Stonewall Jackson's Headquarters Museum or George Washington's Office Museum. Less than a mile from Old Town is the Museum of the Shenandoah Valley, which interprets the art, history, and culture of the valley.

Head south on US 11 and within 10 miles you'll come to Stephens City, which has, among its attributes, an honest-to-goodness drive-in movie the-

You will find wide-open spaces of farmland, as well as attentive cows, along US 11.

ater. The Family Drive-In, just south of Stephens City, has two screens, a playground, and, of course, a concession stand. Family pets are even allowed. The theater operates, naturally, during warm-weather months.

Midway between Middletown and Strasburg, about 15 miles south of Winchester, you'll find Belle Grove Plantation, the magnificent 18th-century home of future President James Madison's sister Nelly. On Belle Grove Road, just west of US 11, the mansion is open for tours. Nearby, you'll also find the headquarters for Cedar Creek Battlefield, site of a critical Union victory in 1864 that coupled with other events helped secure Lincoln's re-election, which had been far from a certainty. Much of the battlefield is on private land and not open to the public, but the headquarters and a couple of monuments are accessible.

Another 5 miles south on US 11 brings you to Strasburg, one of the great little towns along the valley road. Known as the Antique Capital of Virginia, Strasburg has numerous antique shops in its historic downtown, none more impressive than The Great Strasburg Emporium, which houses more than 100 antiques and art dealers, at the intersection at US 11 and VA 55.

By the time we get to Woodstock, another dozen miles down the road, we are ready for ice cream, so we pull into Katie's Frozen Custard, a little stand in front of a motel at US 11's intersection with Fairground Road. The medium cups of chocolate-and-vanilla swirl come piled high with frozen goodness and hit the spot. We sit at a patio table and enjoy the treat as we watch the traffic pass.

US 11 slices through the middle of these towns, the roadway passing a few feet from handsome old homes with rocking chair porches and residents quite happy to offer a smile and a wave. Drive through on a weekend and you might happen upon a street festival or a series of yard sales that beckon you to stop.

Fresh, warm potato chips might just do the same. We continue south on US 11, through Edinburg and then Mt. Jackson. Just south of Mt. Jackson, we turn right on Caverns Road and then make another right on, yes, Caverns Road, before making yet another right on Industrial Park Road, which brings us into a nondescript industrial park, as you might have guessed, and then a sign for Route 11 Potato Chips. If you like potato chips, this stop is a must. Consider it educational, if you must.

Not far from the Route 11 chips factory, you can take a drive through time—and a covered bridge. You find Meems Bottom Bridge, spanning the north fork of the Shenandoah River, on Wissler Road, just west of US 11. At slightly over 200 feet, it's the longest covered bridge still remaining in Virginia. We drive across the one-lane bridge, make a U-turn, and do it again. Built in the 1890s, the bridge was burned by vandals in 1976, and then rebuilt with some of the salvaged original timbers, undergirded with steel beams and concrete piers. So as old bridges go, this one's pretty sturdy.

New Market is next up, a charming little town that, like others along the way, was built right on the valley road. You could easily spend a week or more traveling US 11, stopping at each town, poking around the shops and museums, spending the night, and moving on to the next one in the morning. Civil War battlefields can be found up and down the valley, but the battlefield at New Market is particularly noteworthy because cadets from Virginia Military Institute, some as young as 15 years of age, fought alongside the Confederate army and helped defeat the Union army. In the 1864 battle, 57 cadets were wounded and 10 were killed; the battle remains a proud milestone in the history of the school we will visit in Lexington. You can walk in the cadets' footsteps at 300-acre New Market Battlefield State Historical Park.

I've long been a fan of **Route 11 Chips**, but I'd never had the opportunity to visit the nerve center of the operation until now. As factories go, this one is not exactly mammoth, but it's nice and new and apparently a far cry from where the company began in the 1990s, in an old feed store up the road in Middletown. The popularity of the hand-cooked chips necessitated the move to bigger quarters.

We arrive when they're actually cooking and bagging the chips, so we wander from window to window watching the process (you can't actually go in the kitchen or shoot photos). Seeing chips being made is all well and good, but the big attraction to being here is sampling them. Employees generously put out baskets of the various flavors of Route 11 chips, some of them still warm: barbecue, dill pickle, sweet potato, Chesapeake crab. You get the idea. A hand-lettered sign above a basket containing Mama Zuma's Revenge habanero-flavored chips carries a warning: VERY HOT! Always up for a dare, I try a few. The sign was right. This is where I should point out it's always a good idea to keep a cold bottle of water in your vehicle.

If you're a fan of potato chips, the Route 11 Chips factory near Mt. Jackson is a required stop.

The samples are in the same room with the counter where you can purchase chips, and the marketing ploy seems to work famously. Customers are leaving carrying many bags of chips. We are no different, but choosing among the dozen or so flavors takes a few minutes. I'd be happy to buy one of each, but I'm trying to maintain a shred of dignity and be a model of moderation for the daughter who's with me. We settle on four flavors, buy several big bags, and go on our way. At least two of the bags are open by the time we reach the car. Moderation today; self-restraint tomorrow.

Go 20 miles south of New Market and find Harrisonburg, a thriving college town of more than 40,000. Home of James Madison University, Harrisonburg offers much in the way of shopping, touring, and walking, if you're of a mind to stop and look around. For a quick bite to eat, we pull over at Bar-B-Q Ranch, an old-style drive-in with curb service and a dining room, a couple miles north of downtown. A barbecue sandwich with slaw, fries, and hush puppies is just what I need, but the place also offers more extensive meals, such as country-fried chicken and rib-eye steak.

Less than 10 miles south of Harrisonburg, you come to Mt. Crawford. Cross over the I-81 interchange, go a little over a mile, and turn left on VA 681 at the sign that reads GREEN VALLEY BOOK FAIR. If you like books—and the place is open—you're in for a treat. The fair typically has a half-

Stonewall Jackson stands watch outside the barracks at Virginia Military Institute.

million books for sale at discount prices, but you must check their schedule: the family-run operation opens its doors for only six sessions a year, each lasting about two weeks. Check it out at http://www.gvbookfair.com.

Staunton, at the crossroads of I-81 and I-64, is a handsome, historic town with much to do and see: visit the Frontier Culture Museum, a living history museum featuring reconstructed working farms from the 17th, 18th, and 19th centuries, representing the immigrants who settled the valley and worked the land; take in a production at the American Shakespeare Center's Blackfriars Playhouse, described as the world's only re-creation of Shakespeare's indoor theater; check out Gypsy Hill Park, a sprawling 214-acre municipal park that's a haven for walking, biking, and rollerblading, offering playing fields, a swimming pool, and even a miniature railroad.

Walk down Beverley Street, in the heart of the historic district, and take in a movie at the Dixie Theater, drop in Camera & Palette, a camera shop and museum with hundreds of old cameras and local historical photographs, or grab a bite at a boutique restaurant like Staunton Grocery, specializing in Southern cuisine using local products, or a down-home place like the Beverley Restaurant, where the meals and pies taste like they came out of your grandmother's kitchen.

Or just stroll or drive around town and admire the Victorian architecture, look around an art gallery, and take note of the eye-catching landmark sculptures created by local artist Willy Ferguson: a giant watering can and flower pots at Greenville Avenue and Coalter Street, an oversized open book at the Staunton Public Library, a huge plow at the intersection of Statler Boulevard and New Hope Road, and the mammoth goose-quill pens and scrolls at Beverley and New Streets at the Pen & Paper Shop. To learn more about one of Staunton's most famous residents, visit the President Woodrow Wilson Library and Museum (and birthplace) on Coalter Street. If you're looking for a place to stay, the Hotel Stonewall Jackson, a 1924 palace renovated in 2005 and next door to the Blackfriars Playhouse, might fit your needs.

Lexington, a city of about 7,000 almost 40 miles south of Staunton on US 11, largely revolves around two of Virginia's most venerable institutions of higher learning: Virginia Military Institute and Washington and Lee University, two schools that in some ways couldn't be more different—VMI is a state school in a military environment, W&L a private university where uniforms are something the football team wears—but they have been next-door neighbors since the 1800s.

The **Green Valley Book Fair** started as an offshoot of the Evans' family auction business. The first one took place in 1971 in the family's barn, although it didn't take long for the occasional fair to outgrow that space. The fair is still held on the old family farm, but the books have been moved to warehouse-type buildings totaling 25,000 square feet. The six-times-a-year fair will feature 20,000 to 30,000 titles and a total of roughly 500,000 volumes: novels, history, science, religion, art, cooking, gardening, and shelves and shelves of children's books. Pretty much everything. Even better than the variety? The prices are 60 to 90 percent below retail.

The books are primarily "returns" from publishers, meaning they're new and in good shape, but simply didn't sell. You're not likely to see many current best-sellers, but you might see them in a year or two.

"I think right away we knew we were on to something," says Michael Evans, of those early days with the weekend sales of used books that his father had acquired. "The first one was successful enough that we did it again. It was one of those things that just grew organically. It really propelled itself. We were selling them, so we had to find more books, and in finding more books we needed more room, and every time we found a new source for books we found out we could sell those."

The fair draws people from all over Virginia and the mid-Atlantic, and from around the country and world.

"We know that folks come in a lot from out of state," Evans tells me. "We're not sure if it's planning to come to the book fair and do other things, or if it's planning to do other things and just making sure it's when the book fair is open."

My 15-year-old daughter and I browse the three levels of bookshelves and stacks for a couple hours. Adults sit on benches, reading their newfound prizes; small children crawl under the tables with a volume of *Curious George* or some other favorite and turn the pages contentedly. The place is like a library on steroids. My daughter, an avid reader, picks out an armful of books to buy. As we settle into the car, she beams and describes the experience.

"That," she says without hesitation, "was awesome."

We park our car at VMI and begin our tour of both schools, both of which are happy for visitors to come by. At first blush, VMI is a bleak-looking place with its dull-colored buildings and spartan barracks, but in my years of traveling to schools around Virginia, I've never found people warmer and more hospitable than those who study, work, and teach at VMI. This is a place of great camaraderie and fierce loyalty, which shines through in any conversation with anyone associated with VMI. And as far as settings go, well, looking across the parade ground at the mountains rising in the distance sort of takes your breath away.

Other than simply walking around the post—that's the preferred description, instead of campus—and soaking in the history of the place, the best places for visitors to go include the George C. Marshall Museum, which honors Marshall, a VMI graduate, Army chief of staff, and architect of the Marshall Plan to rebuild western Europe after World War II, and the VMI Museum in Jackson Memorial Hall. Short on time, we are able to visit only the VMI Museum, where among the noteworthy items on display is the mounted hide of Little Sorrel, the warhorse of General Thomas "Stonewall" Jackson, a professor of natural philosophy at VMI. In the same display case, we see Jackson's desk and the raincoat he wore when he was mortally wounded by shots fired by his own men. In the world of odd little facts, Jackson is buried in Lexington, but his left arm, amputated after being shattered by gunfire, is buried in a cemetery near the Chancellorsville battlefield.

We walk over to the leafy W&L campus, marked by stately buildings with large columns. Something else you'll see at both VMI and W&L that you wouldn't have seen in early years are women: once male-only, both schools now enroll women. We hear the hourly chime from the Lee Chapel, which is open for tours, and go there. We sit in the pews where General Robert E. Lee sat during daily worship services when he was school president after the Civil War. (The school previously was known as Washington College, in honor of George Washington, whose gift of $20,000 helped the fledgling college survive.) Lee is buried beneath the chapel, as are his wife, parents, children, and other relatives. His beloved horse, Traveller, is buried outside the chapel. Also beneath the chapel is a small, but splendid museum that features Lee artifacts, including a lantern he used during the war as well as gloves, eyeglasses, and shaving razor and brush.

A walking tour is a fine way to see Lexington. We wander through a weekly farmers' market and a bookstore, and finally over to The Palms, a popular restaurant on West Nelson Street in a building that has previously housed a grain and feed store and an ice cream parlor. A debating club held its weekly debates on this site in the 1800s, and also developed a public library here for the city. The Palms has a historic yet funky feel

Natural Bridge is a natural wonder that actually is a bridge for US 11 traffic.

with its stamped-tin ceiling and brightly painted booths. Ceiling fans turn slowly overhead. The Hot Brown—a sandwich of roast beef, mozzarella, onion, peppers, and bacon on a roll—tops the lunch menu. I choose The Stonewall, which features turkey, ham, and Swiss on a Kaiser roll. My son enjoys the cheese quesadillas, and we share a plate of first-rate onion rings.

Natural Bridge, the last stop on this trip down the valley pike, is 15 miles to the south of Lexington on US 11. Privately owned, Natural Bridge has a somewhat different feel than a state or national park, as it comes with a toy museum, a wax museum, caverns, and a nightly musical pageant called *Drama of Creation*. Before we get to Natural Bridge, a mile north of the town, we come upon something quite unexpected: Foamhenge, a replica of Stonehenge fashioned out of painted foam. We walk up the hillside to this tongue-in-cheek attraction and roam among the pillars of foam. I can't say it's a spiritual experience, but it does make me smile, and the view of the surrounding countryside is striking. Foamhenge is the handiwork of Mark Cline, who has created other attractions, including the nearby Professor Cline's Haunted Monster Museum.

It's late by the time we arrive in Natural Bridge, so we check in at Natural Bridge Hotel, across the street from the entrance to the bridge itself and just before US 11 crosses the bridge itself (though you can't see much from atop the bridge because of fencing). Since US 11 parallels I-81 closely, there is never a shortage of chain hotels along the way. But you also will find numerous bed-and-breakfast inns and one-of-the-kind lodging possibilities like Natural Bridge Hotel. With more than 150 guest rooms, it's a big place with a restaurant on the first floor. Our spacious room has a private porch with a screen door to invite in cool mountain breezes.

Next morning, we walk over to the visitor center to purchase our ticket to see Natural Bridge. A shuttle will take you down the hill to the bridge, but we decide to walk the 137 steps along a pretty path. A paved walkway meanders along Cedar Creek to the bridge: 20 stories of rock carved by nature into a magnificent arch. We stroll beneath the bridge and spot, more than 20 feet above the creek, the initials G. W., which some believe George Washington carved when he came to survey the bridge in 1750. We continue down the walkway, past a re-created Native American village and a saltpeter cave, and then on down the shady path next to the shallow creek. On a hot day, this is a fine place to take off your shoes, sit on a rock, and let the cool water wash over your toes.

IN THE AREA

Accommodations

Hotel Strasburg, 213 S. Holliday Street, Strasburg. Call 540-465-9191. Originally built as a hospital in 1902, it has long been a popular spot for lodging and dining. Twenty-nine antique-filled rooms, some with whirlpool tubs, a pub, and a casual fine-dining restaurant. Web site: http://www.hotelstrasburg.com.

Hotel Stonewall Jackson, 24 S. Market Street, Staunton. Call 540-885-4848. A gracious, Southern hotel in the historic downtown district, built in 1924, renovated in 2005, and featuring a Wurlitzer organ in the mezzanine. Web site: http://www.stonewalljacksonhotel.com.

Natural Bridge Hotel, 15 Appledore Lane, Natural Bridge. Call 540-291-2121. More than 150 guest rooms, fine dining, and cocktail lounge. Within walking distance of Natural Bridge. Web site: http://www.naturalbridge va.com.

Attractions and Recreation

American Shakespeare Center, 10 S. Market Street, Staunton. Shakespeare's works performed in a re-creation of the first indoor theater in the English-speaking world. Web site: http://www.americanshakespearecenter .com.

Frontier Culture Museum, 1290 Richmond Road, Staunton. Call 540-332-7850. Tells the story of the pioneers and immigrants who settled the valley through living history demonstrations and re-created farmsteads. Web site: http://www.frontiermuseum.org.

Green Valley Book Fair, 2192 Green Valley Lane, Mt. Crawford. Call 1-800-385-0099. A book-lover's paradise, with an estimated 500,000 discount-priced books for sale at the fair, which is open for six sessions each year. Web site: http://www.gvbookfair.com.

Museum of the Shenandoah Valley, 901 Amherst Street, Winchester. Call 540-662-1473. Chronicles the valley's art, history, and culture through a historic house, formal gardens, and museum galleries. Web site: http://www.shenandoahmuseum.org.

Natural Bridge, 15 Appledore Lane, Natural Bridge. Call 540-291-2121. Carved by nature from solid rock, the 20-story bridge has long been a tourist favorite. Web site: http://www.naturalbridgeva.com.

New Market Battlefield State Historical Park, P.O. Box 1864, New Market. Call 1-866-515-1864. Site of the Civil War battle of New Market, featuring Hall of Valor Museum. Web site: http://www2.vmi.edu/museum /nm/index.html.

Route 11 Potato Chips Factory, 11 Edwards Way, Mt. Jackson. Call 540-477-9664. Watch chips being made, then help yourself to samples. Also a retail outlet. Web site: http://www.rt11.com.

Dining

Bar-B-Q Ranch, 3311 N. Valley Pike, Harrisonburg. Call 540-434-3296. Old-style drive-in with a dining room. Barbecue, fried chicken, hush puppies. Good service.

Beverley Restaurant, 12. E. Beverley Street, Staunton. Call 540-886-4317. Homestyle Southern cooking with great pies, in the downtown historic district. Web site: http://www.thebeverleyrestaurant.com.

Pink Cadillac Diner, 4743 S. Lee Highway, Natural Bridge. Call 540-291-2378. A 1950s-style diner with burgers, sandwiches, and fried chicken, but also offers a vegetable plate. On US 11 between Lexington and Natural Bridge. You'll know it by the pink Cadillac parked out front. Web site: http://www.pinkcadillacdineronline.com.

The Palms, 101 W. Nelson Street, Lexington. Call 540-463-7911. Casual dining in a friendly atmosphere. Web site: http://www.thepalmslexington.com.

Other Contacts

Shenandoah Valley Travel Association. Call 800-847-4878. Web site: http://www.visitshenandoah.org.

Sugar Tree Country Store is a McDowell outpost for maple syrup.

CHAPTER

13

Mountain Hideaways

Scenery and syrup beckon visitors to western highlands

Estimated length: 150 miles
Estimated time: Overnight or weekend

Getting there: From Staunton, at junction of I-81 and I-64, go west on US 250 to Monterey, south on US 220 to Warm Springs, east on VA 39 and north on VA 42, which will bring you back to US 250 and Staunton.

Highlights: The spectacular beauty of the forested mountains and lush valleys of Virginia's two least-populated counties: **Highland County**, home of maple sugar camps and the annual **Maple Festival**, and **Bath County**, home of healing waters and **The Homestead**. A restful night at the **Highland Inn,** an old country hotel in **Monterey**, and a pleasant morning spent browsing the town's shops and quiet streets. Superb classical music in an exquisite barn-turned-concert hall at **Garth Newel Music Center**. A down-home meal, punctuated with a slice of pie, at **Mrs. Rowe's Restaurant** in Staunton.

The countryside quickly unfolds before you as you leave behind the interstate highways and Staunton and head west into the highlands. US 250 follows the historic route of the Staunton-to-Parkersburg Turnpike, an old toll road built in the 1800s to help open the western frontier by connecting the Shenandoah Valley with the Ohio River. We're not going as far west as the Ohio on this trip, just Monterey, a very small but attractive town and the county seat of Highland County—sometimes referred to as Virginia's Switzerland. I've never been to Switzerland, so I can't really make a comparison, but Highland certainly is pretty enough. It also has a lot of sugar maple trees, but that's getting a little ahead of the story.

The drive between Staunton and Monterey covers less than 45 miles, but the going is slow in stretches when you're climbing or descending mountain switchbacks. You'll appreciate the simplicity of the first part of the route, scenic, two-lane driving through valley farmland; it gets a little more demanding once you leave Augusta County and enter Highland, which has a population of only 2,400, the smallest among Virginia counties. Bath is second-smallest with 4,500 residents.

The road carries you into the George Washington National Forest. A stretch-your-legs-time arrives with a turnoff for the Confederate Breastworks Interpretative Trail, atop Shenandoah Mountain, where Confederate soldiers constructed a trench-like fortification during the early part of the Civil War. Walk a short loop trail that follows the remnants of the trench. From here, you get a striking view of the valley where we're headed. Drive

Shallow rivers running through lush valleys lend beauty to Highland and Bath counties.

through the community of Head Waters, which is Miller's Store, Headwaters Presbyterian Chapel, a few houses, and little more. Cross the Cowpasture and Bullpasture Rivers, near *their* headwaters; a couple of counties downstream, the rivers flow together and help form the James River.

Here's McDowell, a town that was the site of a bloody Civil War battle in 1862. Union troops were moving toward Staunton, attempting to occupy the South's breadbasket, the fertile Shenandoah Valley. Confederate troops successfully repelled them, the victory marking the beginning of General Thomas "Stonewall" Jackson's Valley Campaign. You can walk or drive to different sites where the battle was fought. A good place to start is the Highland County Museum and Heritage Center, located in an 1851 house that served as a hospital during the battle. It also has been a stagecoach stop and hotel.

Near the center of town, you'll find Sugar Tree Country Store & Sugar House, where you can buy apple butter, pottery, and handcrafted toys, but the signature products are, as you might expect, maple related. This is one of the local operations that makes and sells pure maple syrup, made from the cold, clear sap of sugar maples growing nearby. The annual Maple Festival, held the second and third weekends of March, is the county's biggest, celebrating the late-winter rising and running of the sap. If you like pancakes—and even if you don't—you'll love this event.

We drive the day's final 10 miles to Monterey, where US 250 is Main Street, just in time to check into The Highland Inn and run across the street to High's Restaurant before it closes. It's Monday night, and our dining options are limited. (The Inn's highly regarded restaurant isn't open on Mondays.) High's is your typical small-town restaurant with good, substantial food served in a friendly atmosphere. Red-and-white checkerboard curtains adorn the windows. We slide into a booth, and I order the dinner special: hamburger steak with mashed potatoes, green beans, and cornbread. You can't do better for $6.95 My son goes with the chicken parmesan and is not disappointed.

As the sun sets behind the mountains, we decide to walk off dinner. Just a few miles east of the West Virginia state line, Monterey is so small you can cover a lot of it in just a few minutes. No shops are open at this hour, but it's a delightful stroll. Although it's August, the evening air is cool, a most pleasant departure from the flatlands whence we've come. This is one of the first things I notice back at the inn: The windows in our room are open. There's no air conditioning, and there isn't need.

A good place to start—or end—this drive is at **Mrs. Rowe's Restaurant**, a popular dining spot and landmark on US 250, just east of Staunton and within sight of I-81. With good down-home food at reasonable prices, the restaurant has become a celebrated stop, yet, it very nearly never happened.

Mildred DiGrassie, who grew up deep in the mountains in a place called Rich Patch, was a divorced mother of three running a restaurant in the small town of Goshen in the late 1940s when Willard Rowe met her. Rowe had a barbecue place in the not-as-small town of Staunton. But his restaurant wasn't doing as well as hers, so when the two decided to get married, he figured he'd sell his and move to Goshen. He found no buyers, however, so Mildred sold her restaurant and they moved to Staunton.

Good thing. Otherwise, many of us would never have gotten to know the woman who later became known as the Pie Lady, and her tasty handiwork.

In Staunton, she introduced some of her customer favorites—such as fried chicken, meatloaf, and pies—to his restaurant, which they renamed Rowe's Seafood and Steakhouse. The restaurant expanded and flourished and really soared when I-81 was built, just a few hundred yards to the west.

"It's kind of funny how the whole place sort of grew up around us," says Mike DiGrassie, Mildred's son, who now runs the place.

Willard Rowe died in 1972, and Mildred carried on, eventually with a new name because customers began referring to it as "Mrs. Rowe's," which had a nice ring to it. Mildred worked until her death in 2003 at age 89.

"She never retired; she just loved people," DiGrassie says as we talk in a back dining room, after the lunch rush and before the dinner crowd arrives. "She was such a strong personality. She knew everybody. If you sat at that counter more than once, she knew who you were."

She also knew how to cook. Many of the recipes used today at the restaurant (and in the catering business and at a second restaurant in Mt. Crawford) are the same ones she used, although some adjustments to the menu have been made to accommodate customers who prefer meatless and low-fat dishes. Still, the mashed potatoes remain authentic, the macaroni-and-cheese the real thing. The restaurant has published many of her recipes in a couple of cookbooks: *Mrs. Rowe's Restaurant Cookbook: A Lifetime of Recipes from the Shenandoah Valley* and *Mrs. Rowe's Little Book of Southern Pies*.

Before I order a late lunch, I ask DiGrassie about the most popular items on the menu? Baked tenderloin and fried chicken, he says, with coconut cream pie for dessert.

The Highland Inn in Monterey is a country lodge rich in history and character.

A Victorian structure with two levels of magnificent, rocking-chair porches stretching across the front, the Inn dates to 1904, when it opened as the Hotel Monterey, the "pride of the mountains," as it was known. If you close your eyes to envision a grand old country lodge, The Highland Inn might be what you see in your mind's eye. It has high ceilings, pull-down shades, honest-to-goodness transoms, charmingly creaky floors, and a welcoming feel. We sleep well.

"The place wasn't built in a fancy style, but it was built very sturdy," says Gregg Morse, who, along with his wife, Deborah, purchased the inn in 2002. He left a job in hotel management in Washington D.C., to move to what he calls "a picture-perfect little town." The Morses always liked this area, taking drives through the mountains whenever they could, even in winter when most people who don't have to be here, aren't. Just a different view of the countryside, he says: "It's amazing what you can see that the leaves were hiding."

Next morning, breakfast is served in the Black Sheep Tavern, a cozy pub attached to the back side of the inn. Fruit, cereal, and coffee cake hit the spot. With the town wide awake, we take another walk and check out a few shops. At Gallery of Mountain Secrets, we find a lot of good local art and the owner, Rich Holman, behind the counter. I ask him why people come to Monterey. His list includes reading, resting and hiking. Mostly, he says, it's simply a getaway.

"We tell people it's more of a place to be than a place to do," he says.

We drop by Evelyn's Pantry, which carries bulk foods, spices, and, of course, maple syrup. You can also get a particularly good chicken salad sandwich. We wander over to the courthouse—Monterey is the county seat—and take an up close look at the monument to Confederate soldiers, a common sight in counties all over the South. We find antique shops, a craft store, and a barbershop, where, if you're interested in a haircut on Saturday the posted hours are 9 AM–1 PM OR SO.

From Monterey, head south on US 220, but first make a 10-minute stop at the open-air Highland Maple Museum, a replica of an old-time sugar house where exhibits and artifacts trace the history of syrup-making, from Native Americans to today. It's just south of town on the left. If you have the time, you should visit another local sugar camp or two—in addition to Sugar Tree Sugar House in McDowell, others include Puffenbarger's Sugar Orchard in Blue Grass, Rexrode's Sugar Orchard in Hightown, Duff's Sugar House south of Monterey, and Southernmost Maple Products at Bolar, at the Bath County line—particularly if you can go in the late winter or early spring when temperatures creep enough above freezing for the sap, or sugar water, to flow. Some syrup makers use miles of plastic tubing running through the forest to gather the sap in central collection points; others collect it the old-fashioned way, in buckets. All use one style of evaporator or another to reduce the sugar water to syrup.

We have a 30-mile drive south on US 220, along the Jackson River for a ways, to Warm Springs, where you can "take the waters." Bath County developed around the warm, mineral spring waters that bubble to the surface in natural pools and are viewed by some as having healing powers. The Homestead, a legendary resort and mountain oasis that has attracted the rich and famous from around the world, was established before the American Revolution, just down the road in Hot Springs. Thomas Jefferson, as an old man suffering from what he described as rheumatism, soaked in one of these pools, protected then by a wooden, octagonal-shaped building. That connection led to the naming of these as the Jefferson Pools by The Homestead Resort, which now owns them. You can still soak in the 98-degree waters in the original 18th- and 19th-century bathhouses—a woman's bathhouse was constructed in the 1800s—for $17 an hour.

WHO IS GARTH NEWEL? NOBODY.

It's a Welsh phrase meaning new hearth or new home, and it was the name given a property in Bath County when Williams Sergeant Kendall, a painter, and his wife, Christine Herter Kendall, moved here in the 1920s to raise Arabian horses.

That farm is now the **Garth Newel Music Center**, a haven for chamber music set on a serene mountainside, in Warm Springs, just off US 220.

"It's a real heaven on earth for me," says Evelyn Grau, the center's artistic director who shows me around. Grau, who plays viola, came here in the early 1980s as a guest artist. After several years, she just decided this is "where I wanted to be." So, she's never left.

Musicians at Garth Newel Music Center in Warm Springs rehearse in a concert hall that was once a riding ring for Arabian horses.

We sit in the concert hall—the old riding ring—with its wood walls and floors, soaring ceiling, and stone fireplace, sunlight streaming in the large windows that look out onto the countryside.

"It's a very warm sound," Grau says of the acoustics in the hall. Intimate, too. White plastic patio chairs are arranged in rows for the next concert. Everyone has a good seat. Audience members are only feet away from the musicians, who perform on a slightly raised wooden stage. A violinist, cellist, and pianist are rehearsing, talking about crescendos, and playing Haydn. It is a rare treat.

The Homestead is the signature destination in these mountains, with skiing, golf, and horseback riding among other activities, but the hills are full of fine bed-and-breakfast inns and rustic cabins for the renting. Nearby Douthat State Park, 25 miles to the southeast on VA 629, is another option for cabins and camping, plus it has more than 40 miles of hiking trails and a 50-acre lake for swimming and trout fishing.

Our destination today is a place you might not necessarily expect to find on a secluded mountainside: Garth Newel Music Center, a one-time farm for Arabian horses that has been transformed into a sanctuary for fine music. The exquisitely rustic concert hall is a former indoor riding ring. The center fulfills its mission of celebrating chamber music amid great natural beauty through year-round public concerts and education programs. It also serves gourmet meals after concerts.

It's time to turn back toward Staunton by heading east on VA 39, which will carry you, just over 20 miles away, to Goshen, a tiny town on the Calfpasture River. Continue following VA 39 east to Goshen Pass, one of the most scenic stretches of road in Virginia, along the Maury River. You might consider swimming, tubing, or canoeing—or if you'd prefer to stay dry, hiking a trail on the north side of the river—while you're here. Pack a picnic and make an afternoon of it. Rockbridge Baths is another 10 miles to the east on VA 39. From there, turn north on VA 252 and head toward Staunton, 30 miles away, at which point you might want to start the loop all over again.

IN THE AREA

Accommodations

Hidden Valley Bed and Breakfast, 2241 Hidden Valley Road, Warm Springs. Call 540-839-3178. The 1851 home, Warwickton, is an historic landmark nestled in a valley along the Jackson River. Web site: http://www.bbonline.com/va/hiddenvalley.

Montvallee Motel, 54 E. Main Street, Monterey. Call 540-468-2500. Vintage 1950s motel. Web site: http://www.montvalleemotel.com.

The Highland Inn, 68 W. Main Street, Monterey. Call 540-468-2143. Turn of the century country inn. Web site: http://www.highland-inn.com.

The Homestead Resort, 7696 Sam Snead Highway, Hot Springs. Golf, ski, spa. Web site: http://www.thehomestead.com.

Attractions and Recreation

Douthat State Park, 14239 Douthat State Park Road, Millboro. Call 540-862-8100. Web site: http://www.dcr.virginia.gov/state_parks/dou.shtml.

Garth Newel Music Center, P.O. Box 240, Warm Springs. Call 540-839-5018. Web site: http://www.garthnewel.org.

George Washington and Jefferson National Forests, 5162 Valleypointe Parkway, Roanoke. Call 540-265-5100. Web site: http://www.fs.fed.us /r8/gwj.

Highland County Museum and Heritage Center, 161 Mansion Road, McDowell. Call 540-396-4478.

Highland Maple Festival, second and third weekends every March. Call 540-468-2550. Visit sugar camps to see how maple syrup is made. Eat pancakes. Wear warm clothing and boots. Web site: http://www.highland county.org.

Dining

Hap's High's Restaurant, 73 West Main Street, Monterey. Call 540-468-1601. Café with home cooking.

Mrs. Rowe's Restaurant, 74 Rowe Road, Staunton. Call 540-886-1833. Southern cooking, including great pies, in a family setting. Web site: http://www.mrsrowes.com.

Stonewall Grocery, 31 Doe Hill Road, McDowell. Call 540-396-4811. Great sandwiches.

Waterwheel Restaurant, at the Inn at Gristmill Square. Old Mill Road, Warm Springs. Call 540-839-2231. Elegant country setting. Web site: www.gristmillsquare.com.

Cucci's at the Varsity Italian Restaurant, 11129 Sam Snead Highway, Hot Springs. Call 540-839-4000. Spaghetti, lasagna, pizza.

Other Contacts

Bath County Chamber of Commerce, P.O. Box 718, 2696 Main Street, Hot Springs. Call 540-839-5409. Web site: http://www.discoverbath.com.

Highland County Chamber of Commerce, P. O. Box 223, Monterey. Call 540-468-2550. Web site: http://www.highlandcounty.org.

14

Garden Spot

Encircled by mountains, Burke's Garden is an out-of-the-way paradise

Estimated length: 75 miles
Estimated time: 2 days

Getting there: From the intersection of I-77 and I-81 near Wytheville, take I-77 north through Big Walker Mountain Tunnel to Exit 64, Rocky Gap, and go south on VA 61.

Highlights: A visit to **Burke's Garden**, Virginia's highest valley, where you find lots of cows and, at **Lost World Ranch,** camels. History and heritage at the **Historic Crab Orchard Museum** in Tazewell. A tribute to the way farm life used to be—and still is—at **Thistle Cove Farm**. Incomparable dining in a cheerfully funky atmosphere at **Cuz's Uptown Barbecue**, which provides a fine place to sleep, too. And you get to drive through the earth in **Big Walker Mountain Tunnel**.

There's nothing particularly backroad-ish about I-77 as it hurtles between mountains through Southwest Virginia. However, what's intriguing about the highway to my 12-year-old son, who's accompanying me on this leg of my statewide journey, is when it goes *through* a mountain as it

LEFT: The roads and farmland stretches from mountain to mountain in Burke's Garden.

does at Big Walker Mountain Tunnel, a few miles south of the town of Bland. Now, that's cool. So, that's where our journey begins.

Big Walker Mountain Tunnel was an engineering marvel when it opened in 1972, and it's still pretty remarkable. It's 4,200 feet long and took five years to build at a cost of $50 million, at the time the most expensive single project undertaken on the Virginia interstate system. All that, and you can change lanes inside it, too, which is unusual for a tunnel.

Drive another 20 miles north and you can do it all over again at BWMT's cousin, the 5,400-foot-long East River Mountain Tunnel, near Bluefield at the Virginia-West Virginia line. But that's past our turnoff at Rocky Gap, where we catch VA 61, a pretty 20-mile drive that will carry us to the turnoff at VA 623 for Burke's Garden.

Known as God's Thumbprint, Burke's Garden is a bowl-shaped valley created long ago when a mountain collapsed, leaving a huge oval depression. The Garden, as locals call it, is 9 miles long, 5 miles wide, more than 3,000 feet above sea level, and accessible by only one paved road: VA 623, steep and twisting as it climbs over the mountain from Tazewell, the nearest town. Lush and fertile, The Garden is a farming community of about 200 full-time residents and maybe 50 more who have weekend or summer homes. Signposts near the entrance to the valley provide the names of those who live here year-round with distances and directions to their homes. The phone directory is a single sheet of paper, and community potluck suppers are commonplace. The sign over the front door of the old post office says simply, GOD'S LAND.

This also is the kind of place it is.

"Yesterday, I walked with the kids to the mill dam, climbing the rocks on the edge of the pond, picking Queen Anne's Lace, and watching the water tumble into a hypnotic swirl beneath the bridge; it was very affordable therapy," Charlotte Whitted tells me. Her family runs Weatherbury Station, a 60-acre farm in The Garden. She's also executive director of the Historic Crab Orchard Museum and Pioneer Park in Tazewell, and a singer/songwriter as well. "All my workday stress just washed with the water straight through the Gap. After chatting with several neighbors that drove or biked by, we all raced for the front yard hammock."

Several roads meander through The Garden. Take any of them, and enjoy the scenery: the long, empty straightaways, the wide-open pastures, and the seamless mountain backdrops. Don't worry. You won't get lost. At some point, all of the roads simply end. Just be careful. You never know when you might encounter a herd of cows crossing the road. They have the right-of-way here. If you're feeling particularly adventurous, you might consider following VA 623 across the valley floor to the other side, where it meets a gravel road that will lead up to the Appalachian Trail. The ridge-line hiking trail reveals a series of unmatched views of the valley.

The valley is named for James Burke, a member of a 1748 survey team who camped in the area and left potato peelings. Burke returned a year later to find a crop of potatoes waiting for him. Native Americans hunted the valley for centuries, but European pioneers didn't settle here until the 1800s. According to local legend, the Vanderbilt family thought The Garden so beautiful they wanted to construct a family castle. But local landowners declined to sell, and the Vanderbilts settled for building Biltmore, America's largest home, in Asheville, North Carolina.

A warning: There's usually not a lot of excitement in The Garden, except when an occasional pig escapes into the neighbor's corn. Stop for a cold drink, a sandwich, and a Burke's Garden ball cap at the Burke's Garden General Store. Or in the winter, you might find locals gathered around the potbellied stove sharing the news of the valley. That's about it. The Garden does have a bed-and-breakfast inn—Liberty Gardens—but there are no restaurants, no grocery stores, no schools (the kids attend the schools in Tazewell). *Gardenties* even lost their post office when the long-time postmaster died. What you get when you come to The Garden is a glimpse of a different sort of life in a different sort of place. It's great for sight-seeing and wonderful for biking.

And they do have camels. The Lost World Ranch is home to several dozen Bactrian camels, the ones with two humps. They're rare in North America, so imagine the probability of finding them in a hemmed-in valley in rural Southwest Virginia. But find them we do.

Head out of The Garden the way you came in and make your way to the Historic Crab Orchard Museum and Pioneer Park, just west of Tazewell, about 17 miles to the west on US 19/460. The museum preserves and promotes Appalachian cultural heritage, depicting life on the American frontier from the viewpoint of pioneers and Native Americans. The museum is built on the Big Crab Orchard archaeological site where American Indians lived and hunted for thousands of years. The first European settlers arrived in 1770 and named the place because of the abundance of wild crabapple trees.

The museum features exhibits of unearthed pottery and tools, as well

I am standing at a fence watching my 12-year-old son ride a camel called Newt, named for a character in *Lonesome Dove,* Jurgelski says. Newt seems nice enough, and he seems positively overjoyed when I turn down his handler's invitation to ride him, too.

We are at **Lost World Ranch**, a little slice of paradise in a bigger slice of paradise. Dr. Bill Jurgelski, the ranch owner, is the camel man of Burke's Garden. An emergency-room physician, Jurgelski purchased the ranch to raise llamas, but he added the double-hump, Bactrian camels—native to the high deserts of China, Mongolia, and Russia—after seeing them on a visit to an exotic animal farm.

"They came over to me and nuzzled my face," he says. "I just fell in love with them."

At the time of our visit, he has more than 40 camels. He breeds them, but can't bring himself to sell them. "It's irrational, but I can't part with any of them," he says with a laugh.

Jurgelski hires out the camels for fairs, petting zoos, and parades. He plans to open the ranch for visitors who'd like to see the camels and maybe even ride them. After my son's ride, Jurgelski's head wrangler of camels and llamas, Jerry Conner, kindly shows us around in a

Bactrian camels give Lost World Ranch an otherworldly feel.

little all-terrain vehicle. We drive into one of the camel yards. Camels are quite large, the biggest of this group weighs more than a ton. They also apparently are curious. They gather around and stick their substantial snouts into the vehicle. It's all I can do to keep from being kissed. Someone mentions the camels have a tendency to spit. Oh, good.

But the camels take pity on us, and we remain dry. Conner, who went to school to learn how to train camels, says they are pretty nice critters.

"I tell you what," he says, "I've had more fun doing this job than anything else I've ever done."

*Historic Crab Orchard Museum and Pioneer Park near Tazewell preserves
Appalachian cultural heritage.*

as displays of mining, medicine, and music. We wander over to see what
I've heard are the two most popular items in the museum: The Varmint and
Old Hitler. Both are stuffed. The Varmint is a notorious coyote that killed
scores of sheep in Burke's Garden before being shot in the 1950s. Old Hitler
was a black bear that caused the same sort of havoc a few years earlier.

Outside, we find more than a dozen log cabins and stone structures—
all original and dating to the early 1800s—which offer an up close view of
life during pioneer days and serve as a perfect stage for the museum's living history programs. Which brings us to Bud Thompson and Don Hagy.
Thompson is a blacksmith, hammering away on an anvil as he stokes the
coal-fired forge in his shop. Hagy, a descendant of the first European settlers to come here, is dressed like a pioneer and holding a long rifle. Both
men are volunteers who entertain and educate visitors and school groups.

"During the 1700s, the smith was probably the most important crafts-
man," says Thompson, who actually used to shoe horses. Today, he shows
us how he makes a horseshoe, but only for a souvenir. He hammers and
bends the red-hot chunk of iron, submerges it in a whisky barrel of cool

water, and then repeats the process until attaining the shape he wants. A good-humored man, he weaves history and tall tales into the conversation as he works.

Hagy tells good stories, too. He shows us how to fire a flintlock rifle, and mentions he's made about 40 guns over the years, plus a couple of cannon. I'm impressed. I've never met anyone who's built a cannon. I think I want to be his friend.

We roam around the rest of the park, which includes a smokehouse, a

Blacksmith Bud Thompson hammers a horseshoe into shape at Historic Crab Orchard Museum and Pioneer Park.

cobbler's shop, a springhouse, an apple house, and a family dwelling. We peek in a large barn and see a Model T Ford, replicas of the McCormick reaper, and a horse-drawn hearse. Every spring, the museum hosts "Skirmish at Jeffersonville," a big Civil War reenactment.

Back on US 19/460, we head southwest toward Pounding Mill and one of my favorite places: Cuz's Uptown Barbecue, a place that almost defies description except to say the art is eye-catching and the food is excellent. It's about a 10-mile drive, but you'll know when you arrive: Just look for the brick silo, the red barn, and the weathervane on the roof that looks like a pig. It is. The two, bigger-than-life cement pigs next to the silo, painted sky blue and fire red, also will confirm you've arrived.

Walk inside and the place dazzles with quirkiness: wall murals of fish and pigs, superhero figures, a Richard Nixon mask, a bronze hippo, Chinese lanterns, and lots more. It's a feast for the eyes—and the appetite. I sample the deep-fried catfish, barbecued pork ribs, and homemade bread before my dinner arrives: prime rib with burgundy gravy. Even the beer tastes colder here. My son loves the made-from-scratch macaroni and cheese, although he elects not to go with the "skanky" version—as the menu puts it—that is prepared with blue cheese. Neither of us, sadly, has room for the French silk chocolate pie.

We're staying the night at Cuz's, in one of the two cabins on the hilltop behind the restaurant. Our cabin has a loft bedroom, a whirlpool tub, and a stone fireplace. In the morning, I make a pot of coffee and enjoy it on the porch that looks across a hillside covered in wildflowers. The restaurant and the highway are in the distance, below us. Cows graze in the next pasture. A creek trickles past the cabin. A low cloud hugs the mountain behind us. I pour a second cup.

For a side trip, drive over to Thistle Cove Farm, the last remaining 30 acres of a family farm that dates to before the Civil War. It's in the dazzlingly pretty section of Tazewell County known as The Cove where the 50th-anniversary movie, *Lassie,* was filmed. The valley has been farmed generally the same way since the 1700s, and, in some cases, by the same families. It's no different at Thistle Cove Farm where Dave and Sandra Bennett raise American Curly horses and Romney and Shetland sheep. The Bennetts operate a "no kill, low-stress farm," and they believe that's part of the reason their sheep produce such high quality wool. The sheep are sheared on a Saturday every April, and the public is invited, though call ahead to determine the date.

Mike and Yvonne Thompson have been running **Cuz's** since 1979, when they converted an old dairy barn into a restaurant. The place has been an institution ever since, or, in the words of author Lee Smith, a native of this part of Virginia and a regular customer: "A masterpiece."

Mike is a local boy, the great-nephew of Virginia Governor George C. Peery, for whom the highway in front of the restaurant is named. He attended boarding school and, in college, majored in art history. Yvonne was born in Hong Kong and came to the United States as a teen, working in an uncle's restaurant before earning a journalism degree. Her first newspaper job was at the paper in the next town over from Pounding Mill. "Cuz" is the long-ago friend who first suggested they turn Mike's family's idle dairy barn into something useful.

There's an upbeat vibe in the dining room, a happy buzz as people eat and visit with one another. Customers come from all over the Southeast and from all walks of life: Millionaires who can fly a helicopter in for dinner and blue-collar folks who live just down the road. But few come as far as some of the specialty food that's flown in: oysters from Massachusetts, ostrich from the Midwest, fish from Hawaii. Why go to the trouble?

Says Mike, "Historically, Southwest Virginia has been perceived as the lesser part of the state. By God, I just wanted to show them how it was done."

The Thompsons have survived two major fires, the last in 2008, largely because of the loyalty of their customers and their staff, some of whom have worked at Cuz's almost since the place opened.

As we sit at the bar, Mike says, "There's a huge obligation to keep it rolling."

Same deal for touring the farm. The Bennetts are glad to have you, but plan ahead. "Farm tours are by appointment as this is a working farm," says Sandra Bennett, "and there's always a chance I'll be working in one of the outer pastures or at the feed store."

IN THE AREA

Accommodations

Cuz's Uptown Barbecue and Cabins, 15746 Governor George C. Peery Highway, Pounding Mill. Fun restaurant with innovative menu. Hillside

cabins. Call 276-964-9014. Restaurant is open March through November.
Web site: http://www.cuzs.us.

Liberty Gardens, Banks Ridge Road, Burke's Garden. Call 276-472-2745.
Bed-and-breakfast inn, in an historic farmhouse.

Attractions and Recreation

Historic Crab Orchard Museum and Pioneer Park, 3663 Crab Orchard
Road, Tazewell. Call 276-988-6755. Tribute to Appalachian cultural heritage. Web site: http://www.craborchardmuseum.com.

Lost World Ranch, P.O. Box 464, Burke's Garden. Call 276-472-2347.
Visit and ride Bactrian camels. Web site: http://www.lostworldranch.com.

Thistle Cove Farm, R.R. 1, Box 351, Tazewell. Call 276-988-4121. A
working Appalachian homestead. American Curly Horses. Romney,
Merino, and Shetland sheep. Farm tours by appointment. Costumed
interpreters focus on Appalachian heritage, Civil War, and agriculture.
Sheep-shearing day every spring is open to the public. Other special
events. Web site: http://www.thistlecovefarm.com.

Dining

Main Street Café, 208 E. Main Street, Tazewell. Call 276- 979-8200. Great
for soups, salads, and sandwiches.

Yong's Cuisine, 105 E. Main Street, Tazewell. Call 276-988-0718. Upscale
dining with excellent steaks, seafood, pasta, and Korean delights.

Other Contacts

Tazewell County, 108 East Main Street, Tazewell. Call 276-988-1200. Web
site: http://www.tazewellcounty.org/tourism/broch1.html.

You can find food, flowers, and fun at the Saturday morning Goochland Farmers Market on the grounds of Grace Episcopal Church.

CHAPTER 15

Going Nowhere in Particular

But you'll always turn up something good on VA 6

Estimated length: 90 miles
Estimated time: 5 hours

Getting there: Just west of Richmond, from intersection of VA 288 and VA 6, go west.

Highlights: Soothing drive through the small towns and rolling country-side of Virginia's piedmont. Coffee and muffins at **Javajodi's Coffee Café** in **Goochland**. Lunch at **Country Blessing's** in **Scottsville**, which also boasts the **Scottsville Museum** and **Canal Basin Square**. VA 6 ends at **Afton**, a village near the starting point for the **Blue Ridge Parkway** going south or the **Skyline Drive** going north. Punctuate the end of the drive with a stop at one of several wineries in the Afton area, or at **Blue Mountain Brewery and Hops Farm**.

When you head west on VA 6 from Richmond, you might well have a particular destination in mind: a winery, perhaps, or a river town like Scottsville where you can get a bite to eat, or paddle a canoe on the James, or maybe you just want a different, slower, more interesting route to the Blue Ridge Parkway. Or maybe, just maybe, you want to take a nice country drive, go where the road takes you, and stop when the mood strikes. VA 6 is that kind of road.

As we depart on a Saturday morning, we have no particular destination in mind, except the end of the road at Afton, 90 miles away, in the Blue Ridge Mountains. We start just west of the interchange with VA 288, an interstate-like highway that slices through the western suburbs of Richmond and across VA 6, known locally as Patterson Avenue. The four-lane road soon shrinks to two, as we roll past volunteer fire departments, a golf course, and sprawling, upscale neighborhoods. We haven't been driving long when we come to The North Pole—the restaurant in Crozier, not Santa's wonderland at the top of the world. The restaurant has a long history here and a reputation for good food and live music, but it's a little early in the day for steak or seafood or even homemade pasta, so we press on.

The road opens up beautifully into rolling pastureland as we pass farms and occasional gated estates and at least one surrounded by razor wire. Welcome to the James River Correctional Center, in what must be the prettiest setting for a prison anywhere. Maintain a safe speed as you drive through. A couple of miles down the road, we come upon another restaurant with a good reputation: Tanglewood Ordinary Restaurant, which serves family-style meals in a log building that was once a dance hall. The menu? Fried chicken, country ham, homemade mashed potatoes, buttermilk biscuits—JUST LIKE GRANDMOTHER'S SUNDAY DINNER, the sign says. Sounds beyond good, but it's barely breakfast time. This requires a return visit.

We come to the town of Goochland, the county seat, and find a spa salon, a butcher shop, and the Goochland Farmers' Market, which sets up Saturday mornings, May through October, on the grounds of Grace Episcopal Church. We browse the stands of fresh fruits and vegetables, baked goods, herbs, flowers and plants, and handmade clothing and crafts. Children run around and play beneath the shade trees of the church, established in the late 1800s, creating a wonderful, festival-like atmosphere.

We walk over to Javajodi's Coffee Café, a converted old-time filling station that looks like an inviting place with rocking chairs on the front porch, and is. Inside, flags of the world serve as window curtains, while license plates and local art adorn the "center-line" yellow walls. The tin ceiling is painted purple. Some of the windows came from a church that was remodeling; the disco ball—yes, the disco ball—hangs from the engine winch from the original garage. Patrons can sit at tables or on comfortable sofas. A group across the room spontaneously breaks into "Happy Birthday." I like this place.

We get coffee, juice, and muffins, and sit awhile to enjoy the atmosphere. The sandwiches and salads we see indicate this would be a fine lunch spot, too. Live music some evenings, as well.

A bateau celebrates old-time river travel at Canal Basin Square in Scottsville.

We move ahead through little crossroads communities like Georges Tavern and small towns like Columbia. You can put in a kayak or canoe at various boat landings along the river at places such as Columbia, Cartersville, and West View, and river outfitters in almost every town are happy to oblige if you need gear or a ride. We don't have a canoe handy when we reach Columbia, but we want to take a good look at the river so we turn left on Columbia Road and cross the bridge over the James. We admire the view for a few minutes before returning to Columbia and continuing westward.

In 6 miles, we come to Fork Union, home of Fork Union Military Academy, and 16 miles later it's Scottsville, a handsome town on a horseshoe bend in the James; in the 1800s it developed as the chief port above Richmond for freight and passenger boats. We stop to explore, first at Canal Basin Square, a little outdoor park that depicts the history of flat-bottom bateaux and packet boat travel. The park is on the site of the original Kanawha Canal Basin.

Across the street, we visit the Scottsville Museum, housed in an 1800s church building. The museum presents the town's history with a sweetly down-home feel, with artifacts like dollhouses, clothes, and old toasters, as well as stories contributed by the community.

Here's the kind of place it is: As we study an exhibit about the effect World War II had on the town and its families, I notice a display about Gilbert Johnson, a young Scottsville resident who was killed in combat in 1945. "He saw his baby girl, Jill, only once when home on leave," an accompanying newspaper story says. Then I meet Jill. She is standing just a few feet from me, intently studying the exhibit herself.

"He was killed when I was nine months old," says Jill Johnson Harwood, who now lives in Jamestown, North Carolina, and just happened to be visiting the museum. "I lived in Scottsville until I was three years old."

We sit down on an old church pew, as she opens a binder of letters from her father to show me. What is she thinking, I ask, as she sees her father memorialized in a museum?

"Happy and sad, different things," she says. "I wish I'd known him. I think a lot about what he would have been like."

But she adds this: "When I saw him on that pedestal, it made me real proud."

Admission to the museum is free. Moments like this are priceless. Be sure to leave a donation.

We stroll through town, window-shopping at an outdoors store and noticing, down the street, a sign for SPACE, which we find out stands for Scottsvillians Promoting Arts, Community, and Education. It's a community group of local residents with different interests who get together for programs on yoga, massage, art, entertainment, and cooking demonstrations. Sounds fun, but we turn our attention to finding a place for lunch. We consider several strong possibilities on Valley Street, the main commercial avenue, and settle on Country Blessing's, a grocery and café that specializes in locally grown and produced food. I order a Horseshoe Bend, a gyro that's quite good; my daughter goes for The Bateau, a sandwich with a couple kinds of ham on a baguette. Relaxing place. Big windows looking out onto the town. Comfy couches. The dining area also is among the shelves of local honeys and jams and six-packs of beer brewed nearby. This gives me an idea for an upcoming stop: Blue Mountain Brewery and Hops Farm.

Just outside Scottsville, you might consider taking a short ride across the James on the Hatton Ferry, one of the last-known hand-poled ferries in America, a relic from a bygone era. Cut loose by the state in 2009 because of budget shortfalls, the free ferry has been running short of funds, but community activists have been trying to keep it alive.

Then continue heading west on VA 6. Near Schuyler, fans of *The Waltons* television series will be unable to contain themselves when they find Walton's Mountain Museum is but a couple of miles off VA 6 down VA 800, also known as Schuyler Road. Housed in the community's former schoolhouse, the museum features replicas of John-Boy's bedroom and Ike Godsey's store, as well as re-creations of the kitchen and living room of the TV series stage set. Earl Hamner, who created the storyline, grew up in a home across the street.

We are in the mountains now, having left the relative flatlands of the James behind in Scottsville. We share the road, briefly, with US 29, before returning to our two-lane climb to Afton. Just before Greenfield, you meet VA 151, the road to Nellysford and eventually Wintergreen Resort. If you turn left on VA 151 and head south for 3 miles, you'll come upon Basic Necessities, a small, unpretentious café, wine, and cheese shop in Nellysford. The shop, which strives to offer "a taste of Europe in the Blue Ridge Mountains," has been described as the finest world-class wine shop in Virginia. It's a favorite among locals, skiers, and anyone else who likes fine wines at good prices, imported cheeses, and fresh-baked bread.

The terrain rises into the hills as VA 6 heads toward Afton Mountain.

As you near the end of the road, reward yourself with a visit to one of several wineries in the Afton area:

Afton Mountain Vineyards, Cardinal Point Vineyard & Winery, Flying Fox Vineyard, Veritas Winery, or, earlier near Faber, DelFosse Vineyards and Winery. I decide, though, to stop at Blue Mountain Brewery, just over a mile north of Avon, where VA 6 turns to the northwest, and just short of Afton. We stay on VA 151 and find the brewery ahead on the right. We could take a tour of the brewery, order a bratwurst from the kitchen, or enjoy a brew in the tasting room, but all I really want is beer for later in the evening when I'm safely off the road, so I purchase a six-pack of Blue Mountain Classic Lager.

For a trip that started out with no particular destination, it certainly concludes with a most purposeful end.

IN THE AREA

Accommodations

Brightly Bed and Breakfast, 2844 River Road West, Goochland. Call 804-556-5070. Home is an 1800s house, surrounded by gardens and fields, with access to exercise room and sauna. Web site: http://www .brightlybandb.com.

High Meadows Vineyard Inn, 55 High Meadows Lane, Scottsville. Call 434-286-2218. A combination of two 1800s houses with accompanying vineyard. Web site: http://www.highmeadows.com.

The White Pig Bed and Breakfast, 5120 Irish Road, Schuyler. Call 434-831-1416. Lodging and animal sanctuary at Briar Creek Farm, a vegan/vegetarian retreat. Web site: http://www.thewhitepig.com.

Attractions and Recreation

Scottsville Museum, 290 Main Street, Scottsville. Call 434-286-2247. Web site: http://www.scottsvillemuseum.com.

Blue Mountain Brewery, 9519 Critzers Shop Road, Afton. Call 540-456-8020. Brewery, tasting room, light fare. Web site: http://www.blue mountainbrewery.com.

James River Reeling and Rafting, 265 Ferry Street, Scottsville. Call 434-286-4386. Offering self-guided float trips on the James River. Web site: http://www.reelingandrafting.com.

Walton's Mountain Museum, 6484 Rockfish River Road, Schuyler. Call 434-831-2000. A must for fans of *The Waltons* television series. Web site: http://www.waltonmuseum.org.

Dining

Basic Necessities, 2226 Rockfish Valley Highway (VA 151), Nellysford. Café, cheeses, wines. Call 434-361-1766. Web site: http://www.basic necessities.us

A sculpture cuts a dramatic figure against a backdrop of vines and mountains at Veritas Vineyard near Afton.

Country Blessing's Local Foods, 280 Valley Street, Scottsville. Call 434-286-3151. Deli, café, grocery. Web site: http://www.countryblessings localfoods.com.

Javajodi's Coffee Café, 2918 River Road West, Goochland. Call 804-556-7979. Coffee, baked goods, sandwiches. Web site: http://www.javajodis coffeecafe.com.

North Pole Restaurant, 1558 River Road West, Crozier. Call 804-784-4222. Steaks and seafood. Web site: http://www.thenorthpolerestaurant .com.

Tanglewood Ordinary Restaurant, 2210 River Road West, Maidens. Call 804-556-3284. Home-cooked food, served family-style. Web site: http://www.ordinary.com.

Other Contacts

Goochland County Chamber of Commerce. Web site: http://www
.goochlandchamber.org.

Monticello Wine Trail. Director of wineries in the Afton area. Web site:
http://www.monticellowinetrail.com.

Scottsville Community Chamber of Commerce. Web site: http://www
.scottsvilleva.com.

CHAPTER

16

Skyline Drive

Roll down your windows, breathe in the mountain air, and enjoy the view

Estimated length: 105 miles
Estimated time: 4 hours

Getting there: The road has four access points along its 105-mile length: **Front Royal**, near I-66 and US 340, **Thornton Gap**, at US 211, **Swift Run Gap**, at US 33, and **Rockfish Gap**, at I-64 and US 250. Though a haven of wild, natural beauty, **Shenandoah National Park** is a short drive from nearby population centers. **Front Royal**, the northern end of the park, is less than 75 miles from **Washington D.C. Rockfish Gap**, the southern end of the park, which connects to the **Blue Ridge Parkway** to the south, is about 90 miles from Richmond.

Highlights: Skyline Drive, a pleasant, though curvy mountain road, is the only public road in **Shenandoah National Park**, so it's hard to get lost. Go in October, and you can enjoy the turning of the leaves. Plan to make lots of stops at overlooks, visitor centers at Milepost 4.6 (**Dickey Ridge**) and 51 (**Big Meadows**), picnic grounds, and hiking trails, including 101 miles of the Appalachian Trail. Side trips include hiking **Old Rag**, a nearby mountain that is one of the most popular destinations for hikers in the Mid-Atlantic, or **Luray Caverns**.

LEFT: Low, stone walls and long, scenic views make the Skyline Drive one of the prettiest drives anywhere.

Skyline Drive courses over, around, and, occasionally, through the Blue Ridge Mountains. The centerpiece of Shenandoah National Park, the scenic drive was designed in the 1930s as a way to provide Americans who were quickly falling in love with their cars a leisurely drive through the mountains. It is still so.

I've been visiting Shenandoah National Park since I was a child, often on autumn trips to view the changing of the leaves. While fall is a most popular time to visit, summer is great, too. Even winter is interesting, although make sure Skyline Drive is open. Although the park is open, the road is sometimes closed because of inclement weather, and most services are shut down between November and April. A quick note about fees: Since Skyline Drive is in a national park, an entry fee is charged. Skyline Drive is often confused with Blue Ridge Parkway. The roads are similar in that they are scenic, mountain roads administered by the National Park Service, and they meet at Rockfish Gap—the southernmost point of Skyline Drive and the northernmost point of Blue Ridge Parkway. But there is no charge to drive the Blue Ridge Parkway, in many places a narrow right-of-way slicing through private land. One more thing about Skyline Drive: The maximum speed limit is 35 mph, so there's no need to be in a rush.

Now, back to our drive. Skyline Drive was largely a project of the Civilian Conservation Corps, the Great Depression-era jobs program. CCC workers cut roadways, flattened slopes, built overlooks, installed low, stone walls and guardrails, and landscaped much of the roadside with trees and shrubs. Besides appealing to Americans and their cars, the construction of Skyline Drive served two other major purposes: to bring a national park to the East and to present a shining example of success amid the nation's economic despair.

Start at Front Royal and come south. Dickey Ridge, a visitor center with exhibits, a movie, and picnic grounds, comes up at Milepost 4.6. Overlooks pop up every few miles, if not more often. I stop at several coming from the north, shooting photographs at each, admiring the view of the valley below. I am not alone, even on a weekday in October, usually the peak leaf season; the parking areas at overlooks are active as people are enjoying the mountains turn autumn red and gold. The northern half of Skyline Drive offers more waysides for food and gas; the southern has more overlooks. There's no shortage of views anywhere.

As a side trip, travel a few miles west on US 211 from Thornton Gap to the town of Luray and visit Luray Caverns, certainly one of the world's

Frequent overlooks beckon motorists to stop, enjoy the view, and snap a few photos.

most popular natural wonders. A half-million visitors come by every year to tour the massive cave with ceilings 10 stories high. "Hear rocks sing" has been the Luray mantra for years, and you really can when they fire up the Great Stalacpipe Organ in the caverns' cathedral room. The walkways are well lighted. You won't feel claustrophobic. The temperatures are perpetually cool. Plus, you can see intriguing rock formations, like the famous fried eggs. Sunnyside up. Be sure to bring your imagination.

If going underground is not your idea of a good time, Luray Caverns also offers a car museum, a garden maze, and a singing tower—a 117-foot tall carillon of 47 bells, the largest one weighing more than 3 tons. Recitals are held regularly in the warm-weather months.

Back on Skyline Drive, I head for Skyland, at Milepost 42, the highest point on Skyline Drive at about 3,600 feet. It began as a 19th-century resort and is now a motel and restaurant, with a spectacular valley view to the west through the huge windows in the dining room.

"When the sun's setting, the whole dining room will stop," says Peter Bizon, executive chef for ARAMARK, the park's concessioner, as we sit at one of the window-side tables between the lunch and dinner rush. "It's spectacular."

I'm talking to Bizon because I want to hear more about his approach in the kitchen, which includes, besides traditional favorites such as pot pies and fried chicken, dishes such as roasted vegetable risotto, and more reliance on fresh, local products—apples, turkey, trout, and sweet corn so flavorful "you can eat it without butter or salt," he said.

"We want to capture the atmosphere of the Shenandoah," says Bizon, who's responsible for all food-service waysides in the park.

I've stayed in the past at Skyland, which has a cabin feel to it with its lodge buildings set in the woods or perched on the edge of a mountain. Deer roam along roadsides and through the resort, and black bear too are prevalent throughout the park. As a result, you have to be careful with food, particularly when camping. The deer and bears are not alone. One evening on a previous trip, a sleepless toddler and I went for a walk around the property and came face-to-face with another critter: a skunk. We walked very quietly and quickly back to our room.

East of Skyland and well off the Skyline Drive is Old Rag, a popular mountain for hikers. Despite the crowds it attracts, Old Rag is no stroll in the park. The approximately 8-mile round-trip hike to the top of the 3,200-foot mountain is strenuous, featuring rock scrambles and steep climbs. The payoff: spectacular panoramic views. You can access the trailhead at Nethers, off VA 600.

From Skyland I head south for another 9 miles to Big Meadows, just about the midway point on Skyline Drive, and, as the name suggests, a spectacular open, grassy expanse favored by wildflowers and deer. Besides hikes and ranger-led tours, Big Meadows also offers a camp store, restaurant, lodging, and campground. In the visitor center, I walk through a fine little museum that focuses on the not-so-easy development of the park, including unpleasant episodes such as the uprooting of mountain people from their land. I drive to the Big Meadows Lodge, a structure built with stones cut from Massanutten Mountain in the 1930s. It's also a nice place to sit awhile, either inside or on the deck, and take in the valley view.

"I love the solitude of Big Meadows, and the quaintness of the accommodations and surrounding area," says Patricia Kirby, a lifelong resident of Hanover County, just outside Richmond, who tells me Big Meadows is one of her favorite places in the state. "It is so peaceful and quiet there, with many trails to walk and get close to nature. Words do not adequately express what my heart feels each time I go there."

Just south of Big Meadows, you will come to a parking area for Milan Gap, at Milepost 52.8, a nondescript pull-off except it's the trailhead for the Mill Prong Trail, a 4.1-mile round-trip hike that will lead you to Rapidan

Camp, the summer retreat built by President Herbert Hoover so he and his wife, Lou Henry, could escape the heat and humidity of Washington summers. I hiked to the summer White House on an earlier visit to Shenandoah: a winter hike in near-zero temperatures with my son's Boy Scout troop. We stopped to rest and eat our peanut butter sandwiches for lunch on the deck of the Brown House, which has been restored to its 1929 appearance. Of course, you can avoid crossing icy streams and having your drinking water freeze by walking the trail in June instead of January.

Keep going south, stopping at overlooks to peer either west into the valley or east into the foothills rippling toward the coast. Enjoy a picnic or take a short hike. Just watch your time. Stops every few miles will eat up your day. Of course, there are not many better ways to spend a day. Finally, you're at Rockfish Gap, the end of the road. You can go west on I-64 toward Staunton or east on the highway toward Richmond. Or, if you haven't had enough of pretty drives, keep straight and continue on the Blue Ridge Parkway.

IN THE AREA

Accommodations and Dining

Big Meadows Lodge and Skyland Resort, Shenandoah National Park. Call 1-888-896-3833. Historic motels and cabins, and full-service dining in a mountain setting. Web site: http://www.visitshenandoah.com.

On a reasonably clear day, you can see pretty much forever from the deck at Big Meadows Lodge.

Attractions and Recreation

Shenandoah National Park, 3655 Hwy 211 East, Luray. Call 540-999-3500. Skyline Drive is the centerpiece of the mountainous park, stretching for 105 miles from Front Royal to Rockfish Gap. Hiking, camping, and scenic overlooks. Web site: http://www.nps.gov/shen/index.htm.

Luray Caverns, 970 US Highway 211, Luray. Call 540-743-6551. Open every day, tours every 20 minutes. Web site: http://www.luraycaverns.com.

CHAPTER

17

Be Prepared to Stop

Scenic and meandering, the Blue Ridge Parkway is a slow, easygoing drive

Estimated length: 220 miles
Estimated time: 2 days

Getting there: Take I-64 to Exit 99, near Waynesboro, then follow the signs to the Blue Ridge Parkway.

Highlights: Called America's Favorite Drive, the **Blue Ridge Parkway** snakes its way through the southern Appalachians, providing views that deserve to be framed and displayed on gallery walls. **Humpback Rocks**, **Peaks of Otter,** and **Meadows of Dan** offer diversions along the way for exploring, dining, and lodging. **Roanoke** is the largest city along the parkway. Stop at **Chateau Morrisette Winery** for a sip of wine or a bite to eat, or settle into your lawn chair or spread your blanket on a hillside at the **Blue Ridge Music Center** amphitheater for an evening of mountain music. For spiritual uplift, pay a visit to **Mayberry Presbyterian** or one of the other five "rock churches" once overseen by the legendary mountain preacher, Bob Childress.

When you turn onto the Blue Ridge Parkway, as we did at Rockfish Gap—the northern terminus of the road also known as Milepost 0—it's

LEFT: Mabry Mill, near the southern end of Virginia's stretch of the Blue Ridge Parkway, is one of the most photographed spots in the state.

important to keep this in mind: Don't be in a hurry. The parkway is the ultimate Sunday Drive, a leisurely, picturesque experience with maximum 45-mph speed limits, no 18-wheelers, and no billboards, but also—and more significantly as far as safety goes—deceptively dangerous curves and steep drop-offs. Take your mind off the road for too long to admire a view or search for a deer, and you might find yourself in a grove of trees, or, worse, lurching down a mountainside.

The National Park Service provides many places along the road for you to pull off and park and marvel at the scenery. We stop at the first major one we come to, Humpback Rocks Visitor Center, just before Milepost 6, which features a mountain farm museum with a log cabin, barn, and other 19th-century buildings that have been relocated here from nearby home-steads. A short trail leads through the farm that comes alive in summer, and

The mountain farm museum at Humpback Rocks Visitor Center is a good place to stretch your legs and learn about life in the mountains in times past.

The 469-mile-long **Blue Ridge Parkway** is typically the National Park Service's most visited unit. It connects the **Shenandoah** and **Great Smoky Mountains** national parks, stretching from Rockfish Gap in the north to the southernmost point near Cherokee, North Carolina. Almost 220 miles of the parkway is in Virginia.

Construction of the parkway began in 1935, during the Great Depression, as a way to create jobs. Thousands of Civilian Conservation Corps workers built much of the parkway, working with private contractors, state and federal highway departments, and Italian and Spanish stonemasons. The road was completed in sections for the next 52 years, the final portion—around Grandfather Mountain, North Carolina—opening in 1987.

The parkway is a favorite drive for motorcyclists as well as motorists, particularly in autumn when the leaves turn, but besides the beauty, everyone must take note of the descending radius curves that require drivers to tighten their steering as they go through them. Keep an eye out, too, for bicyclists, hikers, deer, and, on occasion, sheep. Keep this in mind, too: During the winter months, parts of the parkway often are closed because of snow or ice.

on spring and fall weekends, with living history demonstrations by park rangers and volunteers in period clothing. On the weekend afternoon when we show up, we encounter a bonus: a local bluegrass band picking on a small stage, as visitors sit beneath a shade tree enjoying the music.

The farm path leads across the parkway to a parking and picnic area for Humpback Gap Overlook and another trail, which accesses the Appalachian Trail. For the price of a moderately strenuous climb of less than a mile to Humpback Rocks, the reward is a spectacular view.

Down the road we come to Love, a tiny community at Milepost 16. We turn at VA 814 and travel a few hundred feet to Royal Oaks Cabins, where we find a gift shop and deli. We select a couple of ice cream bars from the cooler and enjoy them at the picnic table on the front porch before continuing our drive south. The parkway doesn't allow commercial businesses or even signs along the road, so it helps to know where to look.

When you think of the parkway you think of far-off valley vistas, but we also find creeks and lakes to hike along, tucked in the woods alongside the road. Otter Lake, at Milepost 63, is a nice place to stretch your legs and, from the looks of a small crowd with rods and reels on the banks, to fish. The lake is just south of Otter Creek, where there is a campground and a restaurant, and just north of the lowest point on the parkway, just below 650 feet, at the James River. The bridge crossing the river marks the beginning of a big, 13-mile climb to the highest point on the parkway in Virginia: 3,950 feet at Apple Orchard Mountain. The highest elevation on the parkway is at 6,500 feet at Richland Balsam, south of Mt. Pisgah, North Carolina.

After Apple Orchard Mountain, we come down to Peaks of Otter, at Milepost 86, one of the more famous stops along the parkway, with a lodge and lake-view restaurant. At the visitor center, we find a museum and nearby a campground and several trails. The Sharp Top Trail is a 1.6-mile strenuous hike that begins near the camp store and leads to a panoramic view. In the past, we've hiked the 3.3-mile Harkening Hill Loop, which begins behind the visitor center and includes some steep terrain on the way to another superb view. We take a stroll around Abbott Lake, next to the restaurant, which is less than a mile and, just that, a stroll.

Depending on your available time and your sense of adventure, a number of attractions await just a few miles off the parkway:

Crabtree Falls, the highest vertical-drop, cascading waterfall east of the Mississippi River. A trail leads to a series of overlooks for viewing the falls. Leave the parkway near Milepost 27, and head east for 6 miles through the village of **Montebello**. Web site: http://www.nelsoncounty.com.

National D-Day Memorial Foundation, Bedford. Leave the parkway near Milepost 86, at Peaks of Otter, and head southeast on VA 43 for 13 miles to Bedford. Memorial address: 3 Overlord Circle, Bedford. Web site: http://www.dday.org.

Roanoke, the largest urban area along the parkway. Four exits off the parkway—between Mileposts 105 (US 460) and 121 (US 220)—take you to Roanoke, just a few miles to the west. Web site: http://www.visitroanoke.com.

Sherando Lake Recreation Area, part of the George Washington National Forest, two lakes for swmming, boating, and fishing, plus camping and hiking. Milepost 16. Take VA 814 west for 4.5 miles to the park. Web site: http://www.fs.fed.us/r8/gwj/.

Wintergreen Resort, skiing, golf, and lodging. Take VA 664, between Mileposts 13 and 14, and go east 1 mile to the Wintergreen entrance on your left. Web site: http://www.wintergreenresort.com.

The thing about driving the parkway is that you're inclination is to stop at every overlook, walk every trail, shoot pictures at every opportunity. The problem, of course, is if you do that it will take you just shy of forever to reach your destination. Pick your spots. One of the spots we pick is the 4-mile, one-way driving loop on Roanoke Mountain, starting at Mile Post 120. Several overlooks along the way provide views of the city of Roanoke and Roanoke Valley.

Past Roanoke, the parkway opens into farmland with split-rail fences marking pastures dotted with hay bales. At Milepost 171, we reach the turnoff for Chateau Morrisette Winery, going west on Black Ridge Road and then south on Winery Road. Chateau Morrisette is one of two wineries in the neighborhood; Villa Appalaccia, 2 miles north, on VA 720, is the other. I've stopped at Chateau Morrisette in the past to shop for a few

Chateau Morrisette Winery in Floyd County has wine tastings, a restaurant, and occasional music festivals.

bottles of wine in the impressive hospitality center. Tastings and tours are also available. The winery's restaurant is next door, serving lunch and dinner. I have eaten there, too; the food, much of it locally grown, is quite good with offerings such as prime rib, duck, lamb, and shrimp and grits. The wine is good, too, it almost goes without saying. I've never been fortunate enough to arrive when one of the periodic music festivals is held on the lovely grounds. I can imagine enjoying a nice glass of merlot as music drifts across the mountainside.

Now, though, we are heading to Meadows of Dan, but, first, Mabry Mill, perhaps the most-photographed spot on the parkway. The rustic mill, at Milepost 176, couldn't be in a prettier setting, with pond in the foreground, trees surrounding it, and the parkway running alongside it. As long as you stop—you have to shoot a picture, remember?—you might as well take a walk on the interpretive trail, which provides a glimpse into life in these hills in years past. There's also a restaurant and gift shop across the parking lot from the mill.

Two miles down the road, we come to Meadows of Dan, a pleasant village where the parkway crosses US 58, with several shops, a few places to eat, and a candy factory. Oddly enough, a highway bypass was constructed in recent years to sidestep the town, diverting potential business away from a place that has no traffic and no traffic light. You shouldn't bypass it, though, for reasons beyond the fact that even at the height of the summer the nights are refreshingly cool.

"People are kind here," said Janie Stidham, who along with husband, Rhett, came to town in 2004 to open Meadow's Edge Knife Shop & Antiques, surely one of the most extensive stores of its kind anywhere. "They'll call and say, 'I'm going down the mountain to Stuart or Mt. Airy or Galax—and it's a long way down the mountain—and they'll say, 'Need anything?'"

In Meadows of Dan, besides the Stidhams' shop that's in a substantial building that once housed a general store, you can buy groceries and gas—or hand-spun, hand-dyed yarns and spinning fiber at Greenberry House. A few hundred yards east of the parkway, you'll find Nancy's Candy Co., a candy factory and store. They'll be glad to have you watch while they make fudge, chocolates, and other goodies. Free samples, too. Sammy Shelor, one of America's best banjo pickers and a Meadows of Dan resident, and his wife, Sue, oversee the design of a musical-themed corn maze that opens to the public each fall at their Mountain Meadow Farm and Craft Market.

Felecia Shelor got her business start as a child, working side-by-side with her grandmother, selling home-grown vegetables to tourists at **Lovers' Leap**, a mountain overlook a few miles east of Meadows of Dan.

"It was the only income my grandmother had," says Shelor, who, through years of long hours, hard work, and unwavering faith (not to mention good luck and loyal friends), turned that early roadside stand experience into Poor Farmer's Market.

Self-reliance is more necessity than philosophical virtue in Southwest Virginia, where isolation long required residents to grow their own food, build their own homes, and fix whatever was broken—or know a neighbor who could do those things. Shelor exemplifies that approach to life, a life that she truly loves.

"I think we're the last of a unique people, native to these mountains, rough and tough and rugged," says Shelor, who is all of those things but also a world traveler, having visited the Middle East numerous times on mission trips. "We could and did live completely off the land."

Now, she tries to save the land, buying up chunks of it to prevent it from being developed so it will be preserved for her grandchildren and anyone else who loves it the way it is.

"The reason people come here is the absolute beauty of the place," she says, "and the peace."

Felecia Shelor operates Poor Farmer's Market in Meadows of Dan.

Meadows of Dan is on The Crooked Road, the state's designated musical heritage trail that winds through Southwest Virginia.

We will spend the night at a nearby cabin, so we buy a few provisions at Poor Farmer's Market to make for dinner. Private cabins for rent are prevalent around the parkway, particularly this stretch through Southwest Virginia. We stay in one that is owned by Felecia Shelor, who operates the market. She rents two cabins on her farm north of town, plus the loft in a new barn. One cabin is rustic, built of logs used by early settlers near the headwaters of the Dan River, which is how Meadows of Dan got its name. The other cabin isn't rustic at all. Perched on a hill set against a rhododendron backdrop at her farm, this cabin has a kitchen, a bath, a soft bed, and a sweet view of the surrounding countryside. This is where we stay.

We awake the next morning to a cool dawn. I sit on the porch of the cabin, sipping a cup of coffee, watching the sun peek over a distant, tree-covered hill. Freshly mown pastures lie below. Only singing birds and leaves rustled gently by a soft breeze interrupt the silence. I am paralyzed with contentment as I understand why people love this part of the world so much.

For breakfast, we head to town to Shelor's old-style country store, a gathering spot for locals and a destination for visitors, who seek locally grown vegetables, hoop cheese, or fried pies. You can play checkers on the porch and fill the tank at the gas pumps out front. We eat breakfast there: country ham biscuits and hot coffee. We pick up a jar of local honey, too.

If you'd like something more than a jar of honey and you have fairly deep pockets, you might want to consider Primland, a 14,000-acre, luxury resort with golf, hunting, a mountaintop lodge, and even an observatory. Primland is southeast of Meadows of Dan, off Busted Rock Road.

Just down the parkway from Meadows of Dan at Milepost 180, we find Mayberry Presbyterian Church, one of the half-dozen rock churches once ministered by the Reverend Bob Childress, the mountain preacher who brought spirituality and education into the hills and hollows of the region. His life is chronicled in the book, *The Man Who Moved a Mountain,* by Richard C. Davids. Stewart Childress left a business career to continue his grandfather's legacy and attend seminary. He's the pastor at two of the churches, including Mayberry. He's also trying to restore the old schoolhouse on Buffalo Mountain that was the centerpiece of his grandfather's ministry.

"It's a calling," Childress has told me. "I feel like it's something where I can actually make a difference. I never really felt like I made that much of a difference in corporate America."

Just south of the church is Mayberry Trading Post, a general store constructed in the 1890s as the Mayberry post office. We hop back on the parkway and head toward the North Carolina border. Before we get there, though, we pass Orchard Gap, at Milepost 193, where an unusual sort of lodging exists: Grassy Creek Cabooses. Proprietor Donnie Yow converted three train cabooses into cabins (and constructed another cabin that looks like a depot). All have whirlpool tubs and unmatched views of the surrounding mountains.

Now, here's a dining tip: If you're close to Fancy Gap, near Milepost 200, stop at the Lakeview Restaurant, just off the parkway on US 52. There's not much of a lake to view, but the food is great. A family diner, the Lakeview is unpretentious and always busy when I show up. I can't ever get past the fried chicken, which is outstanding. Another tip: order the outstanding coconut crème pie *before* dinner just so they don't run out by dessert time. That happened to a friend once. But it won't happen again.

The hills come alive with country, bluegrass, and old-time mountain music at the Blue Ridge Music Center, an outdoor amphitheater and indoor interpretive center at Milepost 213, just before the North Carolina state line. The music center is operated by the National Park Service and National Council for the Traditional Arts. If you're lucky enough to see an outdoor show, pack a picnic dinner, bring a lawn chair, and find a spot on the tiered hillside. Like the parkway itself, the music center is a no-hurry zone. Sit back, relax, and tap your toes to the music.

IN THE AREA

Accommodations

Grassy Creek Cabooses, 278 Caboose Lane, Fancy Gap. Call 276-398-1100. Web site: http://www.grassycreekcabooses.com.

Peaks of Otter Lodge, 85554 Blue Ridge Parkway, Bedford. Call 540-586-1081. Lodging and dining. Web site: http://www.peaksofotter.com.

Poor Farmer's Cabins, 2616 JEB Stuart Highway, Meadows of Dan. Call 276-952-2670. Web site: http://www.poorfarmersmarket.biz. Other

Meadows of Dan cabins and lodging, http://www.meadowsofdanva
.com/lodging.htm.

Royal Oaks Cabins, 45 Royal Oaks Lane, Love. Call 1-800-410-0627.
With a general store for sandwiches and snacks. Web site: http://www
.vacabins.com.

Attractions and Recreation

Blue Ridge Music Center, 700 Foothills Road, Galax. Call 276- 236-5309.
Web site: http://www.blueridgemusiccenter.org.

Chateau Morrisette Winery, 287 Winery Road, Floyd. Call 540-593-
2865. Wine tastings and tours, and adjacent restaurant. Web site: http:
//www.chateaumorrisette.com.

Mayberry Presbyterian Church, 1127 Mayberry Church Road, Meadows
of Dan. Web site: http://www.mayberrychurch.org.

Primland, 2000 Busted Rock Road, Meadows of Dan. Call 276-222-3800.
Resort featuring golf, hunting, lodging, horseback riding. Web site: http:
//www.primland.com.

Villa Appalaccia Winery, 752 Rock Castle Gorge, Floyd. Call 540-593-
3100. Web site: http://www.villaappalaccia.com.

Dining

Lakeview Restaurant, intersection of US 52 and the Parkway, Fancy
Gap. Call 276-728-7841. Family dining. Web site: http://www.fancygap
tourism.com/dining-and-shopping/dining.

Mabry Mill Restaurant, Milepost 176.2, Meadows of Dan. Call 276-952-
2947. Well known for its buckwheat pancakes, as well as country ham and
barbecue. Web site: http://www.blueridgeresort.com.

Otter Creek Restaurant, Milepost 60.8, Big Island. Call 434-299-5862.
Informal restaurant with country cooking. Web site: http://www.peaksof
otter.com/rest_ottercreek.html.

Other Contacts

Blue Ridge Parkway, National Park Service. Web site: http://www.nps
.gov/blri.

Meadows of Dan, off the Parkway at Milepost 178. Web site: http:
//www.meadowsofdanva.com.

The view from Grayson Highlands State Park, even on a not-so-sunny day, can take your breath away.

CHAPTER

18

The Crooked Road

Fiddling around on Virginia's Heritage Music Trail

Estimated length: 300 miles

Estimated time: A full week, or, better yet, make occasional day or overnight trips to the area

Getting there: The Crooked Road, which largely follows the twists and turns of US 58 through the mountains and valleys of Southwest Virginia, runs between **Rocky Mount** in Franklin County and **Breaks Interstate Park** on the Virginia-Kentucky line. As for getting there, it depends on which end you consider the starting point. To reach Rocky Mount in the east, take US 220 from Roanoke and go south for 25 miles. To reach Breaks Interstate Park in the west, take US 460 west from Bluefield for 65 miles to Vansant, west on VA 83 to Haysi, north on VA 80 to the park.

Highlights: Live music—some scheduled, some not—all along the road in theaters, fire halls, and groceries. Places you won't want to miss include: **Floyd Country Store,** in particular, on Friday evenings or Sunday afternoons. The **Galax Fiddlers Convention** in August, or Galax's **Barr's Fiddle Shop** every day. The wild ponies of **Grayson Highlands State Park.** **Virginia Creeper Trail,** featuring a 17-mile, downhill stretch from **White Top Station** to **Damascus,** and **New River Trail State Park**, a pair of rails-to-trails biking and hiking trails. Shows at the **Barter Theatre** in **Abingdon** and **Carter Family Fold** in **Hiltons. Ralph Stanley Museum and**

Traditional Mountain Music Center in **Clintwood**. The beauty and remoteness of **Breaks Interstate Park**, the so-called Grand Canyon of the South. Breakfast at the **Hillsville Diner**. A picnic lunch at the **Thomas Knob Shelter** on the **Appalachian Trail**, at the foot of **Mt. Rogers**, the highest mountain Virginia. Dinner at **Mosby's Restaurant** in **Wise**.

The Crooked Road isn't an easy drive—it's not The *Straight* Road, after all—but it sure is fun. The banjo and fiddle sound of Appalachian music helps define this region of Virginia, and serves as the soundtrack for the lives of many families for whom music was a great escape and a shared joy in an otherwise isolated existence. Seemingly around every curve of the Crooked Road you'll find something music-related: an annual festival or a weekly jam session, an engaging museum or a luthier's workshop. Wayside kiosks all along the road provide information about the musical contributions of specific areas and, when you tune your radio to the correct frequency, a sampling of picking, singing, and narration that sheds further light on the locality and its story.

Virginia State Folklorist Jon Lohman describes the Crooked Road as a "vibrant center for the continuation of these cherished musical traditions."

"While Virginia is home to an abundant number of excellent driving trails passing through important historic sites, the Crooked Road engages the traveler in living, breathing communities, where traditional mountain music is played with buoyant joy and breathtaking artistry," Lohman tells me. "The visitor to the Crooked Road will see the finest players in the most intimate and relaxed of settings—local jam sessions, fiddlers conventions, and cozy, time-worn dance halls. Whether one is a musician or a toe-tapper, the Crooked Road is, simply put, one hell of a good time."

There aren't many traffic lights along the 300-mile route that cuts through 10 counties, but there are other impediments. Getting behind a rumbling coal truck on a steep, narrow, tortuous stretch of pavement in Dickenson County will challenge your patience and make you adopt an unhurried approach to your driving tour, like it or not. Which is another way of saying: Don't be too ambitious. A map of the Crooked Road lying on your kitchen table looks like a day's drive, maybe two, but don't be fooled. The Crooked Road, primarily two lanes for much of its length, will never be mistaken for an interstate highway, so dial down your travel expectations. Besides, the joy of driving the road is not *driving* the road; it's in the stopping, looking, and listening. Poking around small towns or hiking mountain trails. Enjoying the hospitality of local residents or pulling up a chair at a local diner. And, of course, hearing the music. That's what it's all about.

The best thing to do before driving the Crooked Road is to check out its web site, http://www.thecrookedroad.org, and see what's available when and where you're going. Or call (276-492-2085) and have a free visitors guide sent to you. There's nothing worse than showing up on a Saturday evening for a weekly music jam that was held the night before. And if you want to spend a little time reading up on what you'll be seeing, try *A Guide to the Crooked Road: Virginia's Heritage Music Trail* by Joe Wilson. It's informative, enlightening, and fun.

Let's hit the road.

The Crooked Road connects the dots of major musical venues throughout the region, beginning on the eastern edge 10 miles west of Rocky Mount on VA 40 at the Blue Ridge Institute and Museum at Ferrum College, the official center for Blue Ridge folklore. The institute interprets and showcases the region's folk heritage through exhibitions, festivals, and a permanent collection of recordings, photographs, and documents. The museum is open year-round. Admission is free. The Blue Ridge Folk Festival, a popular event, is held here every October, on the fourth Saturday. The day features music, old-time crafts, and contests involving farm animals, such as herding dogs and jumping mules. There's even a coon dog race.

Before you get to Ferrum, though, you might want to check out Rocky Mount, the sort of small town where you can find live music at a place like Dairy Queen (995 Franklin Street), which hosts a music jam every Thursday morning, September through May. You can't beat bluegrass and Blizzards. Elsewhere in town, you can find similar deals, without the ice cream, at Bernard's Carpet Shop (1696 Franklin Street), where the jams are held on Wednesday evenings after the shop closes, and at Cannaday's Wholesale (19986 Virgil Goode Highway), where musicians and dancers show up on the first and third Friday evenings of each month. Admission is free at all three places.

Floyd, at the intersection of US 221 and VA 8, is the quintessential small town with an old-time hardware store, a one-chair barbershop, and a single traffic light. But Floyd has something else going for it: a vibrant community of musicians and artists, and a spirit that enables a local non-profit thrift shop, Angels in the Attic, to donate more than a half-million dollars to local service agencies in the first 10 years of its existence. Oh, and there's lots of music, mostly bluegrass and old-time mountain music, but also Celtic, jazz, and rock.

The musical hub is the Floyd Country Store, where the Friday night jamborees and Sunday afternoon jams draw big crowds. But you can find live music at places like the Sun Music Hall and Cultural Arts Center, a former sewing factory that has an auditorium, an espresso bar, a Mexican restaurant, and a handmade clothing outlet. You'll also come upon live music at places such as Oddfella's Cantina, a dining spot that specializes in dishes made with locally grown food. But the town's sidewalks seem to be as good a spot as any to find live music. On days or evenings of indoor performances, it's not unusual to find little groups of musicians congregating outside to pick a little and share a tune. There's also County Sales, one of the largest retailers of bluegrass, old-time, and traditional country music. Known worldwide for its mail-order and Internet business and its deep inventory, the County Sales warehouse is just off Main Street and open to the public.

If you can time your visit accordingly, the annual outdoor FloydFest in late July, featuring four days of all kinds of music in a spectacular mountain setting, is a must-do event.

Stuart is a 25-mile drive south of Floyd on VA 8. Named for Confederate General J. E. B. Stuart who was born at nearby Laurel Hill, the town offers musical diversions—such as the weekly Thursday night jam session at State Line Grocery—plus other attractions. Fairy Stone State Park, 20 miles to the northeast of Stuart off VA 8 and VA 57, is named for the rare mineral crosses you can find in abundance in the park. The legend goes something like this: Fairies who once cavorted in the area wept when they received word of Christ's death. As their tears fell to earth, they crystalized to form crosses. The crosses are actually stones made of staurolite, a combination of silica, iron, and aluminum that crystallizes at sharp angles, resulting in the cross-like shape.

Laurel Hill, site of Stuart's birthplace, is in Ararat, about 25 miles southwest of Stuart off VA 8 and VA 103, and the property is open for self-guided tours, though the house itself burned down in the 1840s and was never rebuilt. Back in Stuart, the Virginia Peach Festival is held each August, and the Apple Dumpling Festival in October.

Leaving Stuart and heading west on US 58, you climb higher into the Blue Ridge and at the top of a particularly twisty stretch of road you come upon Lovers Leap, an overlook with a small parking area and a huge view

We walk into **Floyd Country Store**, past the old-time soda fountain and the old-fashioned barrels of penny candy and all the way to the back where we find 13 people seated in a circle playing fiddles, banjos, mandolins, dulcimers, and guitars. Maybe twice that many are gathered around them, listening, tapping their toes, and applauding appreciatively.

This is the weekly Sunday afternoon jam, a time for anyone to bring an instrument and join in. The Friday Night Jamborees are a little more formal, with an hour of gospel music and then scheduled bands and dancing. Sundays are casual. We stand and listen for a while. The performers take turns choosing songs, take turns singing, take turns playing solos. It's democracy with a pick and bow.

The store opened in 1910 as a farmers supply store, and it remained a hardware store or general store and community gathering-place for most of the century. But then during the 1990s it stopped being a store, although it stayed open one night a week for music: the Friday Night Jamboree. Current owners Woody and Jackie Crenshaw have renovated the place and made it a country store

The Floyd Country Store is an old-time general store and a music hall with live shows and jam sessions.

again, selling all kinds of things that you might have found in such stores long ago: toy tractors, handmade dolls, and rolling pins. I'm not sure about the tradition of the potted possum I found on a shelf, but it's $2.75 a can if you're interested. They also have an extensive collection of recorded music for sale, as well as all kinds of clothes. On Friday nights, they roll out the merchandise and make room for the dance floor.

At the lunch counter, I order a barbecue with cole slaw, pinto beans, and a root beer. We sit in a window booth, listening to the music from the back of the store and watching people strolling the sidewalk. It's a fine way to spend a Sunday afternoon.

of the surrounding mountain and valley. It's worth a stop.

As you drive down the mountain, not more than a few hundred yards below the overlook and just a few feet off the road, you come upon a cute little cottage with a sign for Henriedda Crafters: Lovers Leap Birdhouses. Henry and Edna Mickles have been building, painting, and selling birdhouses since they moved here in the 1990s; they live upstairs. I've stopped to see Henry for years, and in 2009 he tells me they've sold well over 30,000 birdhouses, which is pretty amazing considering their shop, at one time a mountain tavern, is high on a rural mountain, not off an interstate highway exit. In fact, Henry says he has customers most every day—sometimes on days you'd least expect it.

"We had customers the day we had a foot of snow," he says with a smile. "Weather doesn't seem to scare them."

Henry started making birdhouses as a hobby and turned it into his livelihood when he got out of the construction business. He says with a laugh he didn't know a crow from a buzzard when he started, but he does now, making all kinds of birdhouses: some are basic-looking birdhouses, but others look like barns, some look like churches, and some look like bird mansions, but all are handcrafted.

Henry Mickles makes birdhouses, lots of birdhouses, on Lover's Leap at Henriedda Crafters.

Head down the mountain, continuing west on US 58, and reach Meadows of Dan, a crossroads with the Blue Ridge Parkway (which we've covered in the chapter on the parkway). From there, it's a 20-mile drive to Hillsville, the seat of Carroll County at US 58's intersection with I-77, and home to the annual Labor Day Gun Show and Flea Market, sponsored by the local Veterans of Foreign Wars post, which draws an estimated 300,000—roughly 100 times the town's population—every year. Music-wise, the same VFW post sponsors a traditional mountain dance every Saturday evening in the spring and summer.

Food-wise, you ought to stop for breakfast or lunch (dinner isn't served, and the place is closed on Sundays) at the Hillsville Diner, a true, old-style diner that's been a landmark in town since the 1940s, when it was towed from its previous location in Mt. Airy, North Carolina. Fast service is one of its hallmarks; reasonable prices another. Friendliness trumps them all. Owner Mac McPeak starts frying the bacon and making the sausage gravy while everyone else is sleeping, so when he opens shortly before 5 AM he is well stocked and ready to roll. Sit at the counter with the regulars and watch Mac toil at the sizzling griddle, scrambling eggs, making pancakes, and carrying on conversations—a maestro of motion—without breaking a single egg, except on purpose.

Next up as you go west on US 58 is Galax, an old farming and factory town that's twice the size of Hillsville, a dozen miles to its east. You'll find "big box" stores here, as well as a number of attractions, most notably the annual Galax Old Fiddlers Convention, a weeklong event of country and mountain music hosted by the local Moose Lodge in the town's Felts Park. Thousands pitch tents and camp for the entire week; others drive in for a day or two. The stage serves as the focal point as musicians compete for cash prizes, but there's just as much music—even more—in the parking lot and campground where festival-goers bring out their guitars, fiddles, and banjos and sit around in lawn chairs and play old, familiar tunes deep into the night.

When the convention's not going on, you can hear live music every Friday night at the Rex Theatre, and in the warm-weather months down the road at the Blue Ridge Music Center and Museum, 6 miles south of Galax. (See chapter on Blue Ridge Parkway.)

Stroll through downtown Galax, stopping in one of the antique shops or maybe Barr's Fiddle Shop, a gathering spot on Main Street for musicians who want to try out one of the handmade fiddles, banjos, or dulcimers, or just chat music. If music makes you hungry, head over to Tlaquepaque, an excellent Mexican restaurant in a nondescript, warehouse-looking building on US 58 just before reaching downtown. I look forward to eating there every time I'm in the area.

If you have the time and you have your bicycle, you might consider pedaling a few miles on the New River Trail, a 57-mile-long linear state park whose southern terminus is Galax. A parking area for the multi-use trail is just off US 58, near downtown. The trail follows an old rail bed, paralleling the scenic New River for much of its length. The trail features two tunnels, three major bridges (the longest more than 1,000 feet), and more than two dozen shorter bridges and trestles. Camping is available along the trail, as well as several access points for parking or arranging pickups or drop-offs, if you don't want to travel the entire trail at once. The trail certainly has some climbs, but you don't need to be a veteran cyclist to do it. How do I know this? My son, when he was six years old and had been riding without training wheels for only a few weeks, pedaled the entire trail over a period of a few days.

US 58 surges westward, following along the New River for a time and then leaving behind a brief segment of four-lane road for the familiar two lanes as it reaches Independence. Fifteen miles from Galax, Independence has a pretty courthouse built in 1908 that doubles as a small museum and visitor center, a Fourth of July parade (of course), and The Davis-Bourne Inn, a bed and breakfast in a magnificent Victorian mansion with a fine-dining restaurant, The Journey's End. Pick up the local weekly newspaper while you're there. It's called *The Declaration*.

Now, the Crooked Road starts to get really crooked. The road rises, falls, and mostly bends through lovely countryside and past Christmas tree farms, one of this area's greatest cash crops. It ventures beyond Mouth of Wilson—home of Oak Hill Academy, one of the nation's best and best-known high school basketball teams—to Volney, about 17 miles past Independence at the Log House Restaurant, where US 58 makes a sharp left turn. If you keep straight, you'll be on VA 16, and you'll miss all of the fun.

If you're short on food or gas, the Log House would be a good place to stop. Options from here to Grayson Highlands State Park, about 8 miles away, are limited. (There isn't anything.) The Log House serves good meals, has a small convenience store, and sells gas. One-stop shopping at its best.

The road to Grayson Highlands includes a fair amount of what I like to call "full-bodied driving." You find yourself leaning into the curves, and there are a lot of them. It's a pretty ride, but you'll be glad when you get to the park, and you don't have to lean anymore. Once you take a look around the park, you'll be even more glad you made the effort to get here. It's one of the most astoundingly beautiful places in Virginia.

If you're lucky, you might run into one of the musicians who makes this area a hotbed for homegrown music, someone like Wayne Henderson. A first-rate, finger-picking guitarist, Henderson lives in the tiny community of Rugby—population of about 7—and has played on stages all over the world, including Carnegie Hall. He's also a master instrument-maker and a great storyteller. Get him to tell you the one about the elephant that escaped from the circus and wandered deep into the hills.

If you're in the area in mid-May, make plans to attend the annual Whitetop Mountain Ramp Festival. Held the third Sunday of May, the festival celebrates the wild leeks that grow in the surrounding mountains. There's music, arts and crafts, and lots of food. You won't want to miss the ramp eating contest that's always highly competitive and entertaining—bottles of mouthwash are among the prizes—but just don't stand too close.

It's only about 30 miles from Grayson Highlands to the next town, Damascus, but it's about an hour ride as the road slinks this way and that through the mountains. Damascus is known as Trail Town for the various trails that intersect here, most notably the Appalachian Trail, but also the Virginia Creeper Trail, the Trans-America National Bicycle Trail, the Iron Mountain Trail, the Daniel Boone Trail, and, of course, the Crooked Road.

Also known as the Friendliest Town on the (Appalachian) Trail, Damascus is a happy sight for hikers who've been in the woods for weeks. They can get a hot meal, a hot shower, and a warm bunk at The Place, a hostel for hikers operated by the local United Methodist Church. If they're living high on the hog, they might spring for a night at one of the town's bed-and-breakfast inns. Every May, the town holds Appalachian Trail Days, a weekend festival celebrating the A.T. and those who hike it, the timing coinciding with when many thru-hikers heading to the northern terminus of the trail at Mt. Katahdin, Maine, come through.

As long as you're here, check out Mt. Rogers Outfitters, on Laurel Avenue (the local name for US 58) and browse among their hiking boots and other gear. If biking's your sport, you have several bike shops in town to choose from. All sell and rent bikes, and operate shuttles to transport bicyclists and their wheels to either end of the popular Virginia Creeper Trail.

High in the mountains, **Grayson Highlands State Park** is a delightful getaway full of hiking trails, wondrous views, and, if you come in mid to late summer, bushes brimming with wild blueberries and blackberries. The juicy fruit slows your hiking, but you never go hungry. The wild ponies will stop you in your tracks, too. A herd has roamed the park for years, and the ponies are friendly and quite accustomed to visitors. They'll even follow you down trails. But resist the temptation to pet and feed them.

The scenery is the real showstopper. Hike the trail behind the visitor center to the Big Pinnacle and Little Pinnacle overlooks, and, in some ways, the alpine views bring to mind the American mountain west, not the typically forested Blue Ridge. But Grayson Highlands is a park of contrasts: Walk Cabin Creek Trail, and find yourself in thick woods, next to a clear, fast-rushing creek. Take off your shoes, dangle your feet in the cool water, and sit a while. If you stay over at the campground and you're fortunate to hit a clear night, walk over to one of the open areas and look up. The stars practically leap off the black canvas of a sky. In fact, stargazing is good just about anywhere in the mountains of Southwest Virginia, far from the light pollution of big cities.

The wild ponies at Grayson Highlands State Park and the adjoining Mt. Rogers National Recreation Area fearlessly greet hikers.

The state's two highest peaks—Mt. Rogers, at over 5,700 feet, and Whitetop Mountain, about 200 feet shorter—are within sight of the park, and both are imminently accessible. My family has hiked Mt. Rogers a half-dozen times, starting at Grayson Highlands, then joining the Appalachian Trail and entering Mt. Rogers National Recreation Area. The round-trip of about 9 miles is a little rocky in spots, but nothing more than a mildly strenuous hike. Take along plenty of water, though. We also pack a lunch, and usually eat our peanut butter sandwiches at the picnic table at Thomas Knob Shelter, an A.T. way station for overnight hikers, less than a mile from the top of Mt. Rogers. A warning: there's no view at the summit; only a U.S. Geological Survey plate affixed to a boulder marks the top. Even without a spectacular view, however, it's still worth the hike: Mt. Rogers is wooded with spruce and fir, making for a most interesting, Canadian-like environment. It's easy to find solitude on the way to Mt. Rogers or on other trails in this backcountry, but not so easy to find a cell signal. Let someone know where you're headed, if even just on the trail registries posted at trailheads.

If you decide to camp at Grayson Highlands, be sure to bring whatever food you want. The park has a camp store for basics, but there's not much in the way of groceries along this stretch of US 58. As far as local restaurants, **Speedy's Chuck Wagon**, a few miles west of the park on US 58, just past the old Mt. Rogers School, is it. Don't be put off by its unassuming appearance, it serves excellent country breakfasts, great burgers, and other substantial fare.

The park's two major events are the **Wayne C. Henderson Music Festival and Guitar Competition** on the third Saturday in June, and the **Grayson Highlands Fall Festival**, on the last full weekend of September. Those are fun and well-attended, but I'm just as pleased to sit quietly by the campfire in the park campground on a cool summer evening.

An easy 15-mile drive from Damascus, Abingdon is at the crossroads of US 58 and I-81. We like to stop at Wildflour Bakery and Restaurant, on US 58 just east of the interstate, in a Victorian-era farmhouse. The bakery promotes itself as having the "best buns in town," and we aren't in a position to dispute it. Since it's morning, we window-shop at the display case of freshly made baked goods and settle on a massive cinnamon bun and a bacon, cheese, and scallion scone. For lunch, the soups are made daily, and the sandwiches arrive on house-made bread. For dinner, the bakery becomes a fine-dining establishment.

Abingdon is a great town with a nice combination of mountain friendliness and artistic sensibility. Nothing exemplifies those qualities better than the Barter Theatre, founded in the Great Depression on the concept of offering entertainment to the public in exchange for food from area farms and gardens to feed the actors. The Barter no longer accepts spinach, eggs, or country hams for admission, but the spirit lives on at the theater that has served as a starting ground for numerous actors who've gone on to perform on the national stage. Today, you can see Barter productions in two different venues in Abingdon: the traditional 500-seat theater on US 58, known locally as West Main Street, and Barter Theatre Stage II, an intimate, 167-seat setting for more intimate productions.

Artwork is on display and for sale at the Arts Depot (314 Depot Square) in an old freight station, and at Cave House (279 E. Main Street), a Victorian mansion that is home to the handmade jewelry, pottery, and quilts of members of a local arts cooperative. Behind the shop, you can see the entrance to Wolf Cave, the residence of wolves that attacked Daniel Boone's dogs in 1760, which explains Abingdon's original name: Wolf Hills.

Coming in the summer of 2011 to Abingdon: Heartwood, a visitor center and gateway for Southwest Virginia artists, featuring retail sales and demonstrations of their crafts. The complex will be situated off Exit 14 of I-81.

Every summer, around the beginning of August, Abingdon hosts the two-week Virginia Highlands Festival, a major event featuring performing arts, crafts, antiques, and more. As for lodging, Abingdon offers a variety of possibilities, from the upscale Martha Washington Hotel and Spa, a one-time women's college across the street from the Barter, to cabins in the country. Because of Abingdon's location next to I-81, a full range of chain motels and hotels, such as the Comfort Inn, is available, too.

Take I-81 south for 15 miles to Bristol, the proclaimed birthplace of country music that sits on the Virginia-Tennessee border. In fact, the state line runs down the middle of State Street. In the music world, Bristol gained its historic standing in 1927 when Ralph Peer of the Victor Talking Machine Co. came to town to arrange the first commercial country music recordings that introduced local musicians such as Jimmie Rodgers, the Stonemans, and the Carter Family to the world.

Live music abounds in Bristol at places such as the Paramount Center for the Arts, the outdoor stage at the Country Music Mural on State Street on summer evenings, and every Thursday night at the Pickin' Porch, in

Once a rail line for trains hauling lumber, iron ore, and passengers, the 34-mile, multi-use **Virginia Creeper Trail** follows the path of the abandoned rail bed and attracts bikers, hikers, and joggers. Named for either the sluggishness of early steam locomotives chugging through the mountains or for a woody vine that grows in this part of the world, the trail runs from the Virginia-North Carolina line, just east of Whitetop Station, to Abingdon. Damascus is the midway point.

The 17-mile, mostly downhill stretch from Whitetop Station to Damascus draws the most crowds, particularly on weekends when the trail becomes quite crowded. You can drive to Whitetop Station, but many people prefer to park in Damascus and rely on one of the town's bike shops for shuttle service to the top. The ride itself requires little rigorous pedaling so it's fairly easy, but you must be careful because you're going down a gravel path on a wooded, mountain trail. The trestles, particularly the 563-foot-long crossing at Creek Junction, add a little excitement.

You easily can ride the trail straight through in less than a couple of hours, but we like to stop along the way at the little gift shop at Green Cove, one of the original depots, as well as at fast-flowing creeks along the way that beckon kids to skip stones or go wading. We've also made a family tradition of stopping for lunch at the Creeper Trail Café in Taylors Valley, a small community about 10 miles from the top. Choose from a nice selection of sandwiches, but I highly recommend the pinto beans and cornbread.

Pedaling the Virginia Creeper Trail, following the path of an old railway line, is fun, scenic, and, particularly on the downhill run from Whitetop Station to Damascus, not particularly strenuous.

The trail flattens for the last few miles into Damascus. Before we reach the center of town, we like to stop for ice cream at In the Country, a shop just across US 58 from the trail. It's a nice way to end the ride. Of course, you're welcome to continue on to Abingdon, which we've done on occasion. That stretch of the trail is slightly uphill, though not exceedingly so, and goes through more farmland than the other half. Just make sure you have a ride waiting for you. Or call ahead for a shuttle.

the Bristol Mall, on Gate City Highway, just east of Exit 1 of I-81. The mall also is home to the Mountain Music Museum, where you'll find displays of vintage musical instruments, photographs, and recordings. Admission is free. There's also a gift shop. Plans are in the works for a Birthplace of Country Music Alliance Cultural Heritage Center downtown.

Back on US 58, we head west toward the far reaches of Southwest Virginia. Instrument-makers like Jack Branch live in the hills and hollows in this part of the state. Branch made his career as a stonemason, but building and selling handcrafted violins and other string instruments has become his passion. He lives on Cove Creek Road, about 10 miles west of Bristol, down a thickly wooded mountain hollow where he and his wife, Nannie, grow their own vegetables, cure their own hams, and make their own wine. We stop by to see Jack and Nannie, among the most hospitable people I've ever known. He shows us around his workshop, he fiddles a few tunes, he tells a few stories. "Every fiddle I've ever made," he says, "the first song I've played on it is 'Amazing Grace.'" The second? "Whiskey Before Breakfast." Jack says come see him.

Twenty miles west of Bristol, come to Hiltons, home of the Carter Family Fold, a performance hall and shrine to one of the first families of country music.

In his home outside Bristol, violin-maker Jack Branch (right) jams with a young friend, Jack Lohmann.

From Hiltons, follow the Crooked Road through Gate City and past Natural Tunnel State Park (see the chapter on the Wilderness Road) to Duffield, where you'll leave US 58 and take US 58-Alternate toward Big Stone Gap, the town made famous by *The Trail of the Lonesome Pine*, a 1908 romance novel by John Fox Jr., and, more recently, by the Big Stone Gap books of Adriana Trigiani. A pleasant town, Big Stone Gap has the Southwest Virginia Museum, a state park housed in a mansion built in the 1880s that tells the story of a region, settled by pioneers, that later developed around the mining industry. On summer evenings, you can attend the stage version of *The Trail of the Lonesome Pine* in an outdoor theater in town.

The Carter Family Fold is all about promises.

"My mom promised her dad when he was dying that this place would live on," Rita Forrester tells me backstage at the Fold, before the weekly Saturday evening show, "and I promised her I'd do everything in my power to maintain what she started."

Forrester's mother was Janette Carter, her grandfather the legendary A. P. Carter, who was involved in the famous 1927 Bristol recordings that put country music on the national map. And what Forrester has kept going is the Carter Family Fold at the **Carter Family Memorial Music Center** on the Carter family's old homeplace at the foot of **Clinch Mountain**. Every Saturday night, hundreds of enthusiasts park their cars and trucks on the grassy shoulders on the side roads near the Fold, and fill the seats of the semi-outdoor hall to listen to good, down-home music.

We arrive on a warm August night, the sides of the ingeniously designed hall raised to welcome any gentle breeze that happens by. Some people sprawl on the grassy hillside outside the hall, enjoying the night air. We take our seats under cover. Before the show starts, we amble down to the concession stand, manned by a small army of volunteers, where the menu includes hot dogs, popcorn, and such fare, but also a weekly special: this evening, it's soup beans and homemade cornbread. My son and I order two specials and return to our seats to enjoy supper.

The **Tennessee Mafia Jug Band**, who mix old-time tunes with good-natured humor, headline tonight's show. People leave their seats to flat-foot dance in front of the stage. Audience members come from all over this region and from states across the country and beyond. One is from Russia, evidence of the Fold's draw as a major tourist attraction in this part of Virginia. At intermission, we walk over to A. P. Carter's birthplace, a log cabin, which is on the property and open to visitors. The A. P. Carter Store, now The Carter Family Museum, is next door to the Fold.

The music here is more than just a catchy tune. It's about family, culture, and pride. Forrester, who works full-time as a university administrator and scrambles in her spare time to operate the Fold with the help of untold volunteers, says she will get tired and discouraged and then someone comes up and tells her how much the Fold and the music mean to them or how it brings back such happy memories of growing up deep in these mountains. Then she knows what she's doing is worthwhile, a promise kept.

Head back to US 58-Alternate toward Norton, where US 23 peels off to the north. Whenever I'm in the area, I like to stop for lunch or dinner at Mosby's Restaurant in Wise. Named for a Confederate general and situated in a stand-alone building in Ridgeview Centre, Mosby's offers an extensive menu of steaks, seafood, and pasta. The place is educational, too, with dramatic prints and portraits of important Civil War participants accompanied by brief descriptions of their war service.

After Wise, proceed on US 23 north for a dozen miles to Pound and turn right on VA 83, which will carry you to Clintwood, home of the Ralph Stanley Museum and Traditional Mountain Music Center, a magnificent tribute to one of the most respected figures in old-time music.

The last 25 miles or so of the Crooked Road include some of the most challenging. We leave Clintwood, continuing along VA 83 toward Clinchco and Haysi, where we will head north on VA 80 for the final stretch to Breaks Interstate Park. The roads through the coalfields are particularly crooked, often framed by a mountain on one side and a creek or small river on the other. There is little wiggle room. Don't go too fast. The aforementioned coal trucks will make sure of that.

Breaks Interstate Park straddles the Virginia-Kentucky border, one of only two "interstate" parks in America, meaning that it's governed by Virginia and Kentucky. About 2/3 of the park is in Virginia. It's been called the Grand Canyon of the South because of the deep gorge cut by the Russell Fork of the Big Sandy River. Breaks has a lot more trees than the Grand Canyon, though, which is something Daniel Boone noticed when he came through in the 1760s, searching for passes through the mountains—or breaks—to the west. The thick forest and the steep gorge, not to mention copperheads and rattlesnakes, encouraged Boone to turn around and find another passage.

We find the woods and the gorge, but, thankfully, no snakes on our visit. Ruggedly beautiful with scenic views of the gorge and surrounding countryside, Breaks is another world for those of us from the eastern part of Virginia. It's a long haul that's well worth the time and miles. We hike along a ridge on a well-marked trail that includes several overlooks. A coal train chugs along far below and then disappears into a mountain tunnel.

The park is remote, but not without amenities. We stay in the Breaks motel, which offers spacious rooms at decent rates with unmatched views. There also are luxury cabins built on the shore of the park's 12-acre lake, rustic cottages, and a campground. On the mornings of our visit, I sit on

In Clintwood, the Ralph Stanley Museum and Traditional Mountain Music Center is a welcoming place and a fine way to spend an afternoon.

We walk into the **Ralph Stanley Museum and Traditional Mountain Music Center** about 3 PM on a Friday afternoon. A sign says the place closes at 4. The genial fellow at the desk—which is the shape of an oversized banjo—says not to worry. "Take your time," he says. "We always say, we'll welcome you in, but we'll never run you off."

We pay our admission and start a self-guided tour of the two-story museum. The building itself is a marvel, a restored, century-old, four-story mansion that in earlier days was a boarding house and a funeral home, though not at the same time. The museum takes you from Stanley's youth in nearby **McClure**, where he learned to sing a capella in the Primitive Baptist Church, to the present day, including when in his 70s he became a national sensation for his high, lonesome sound in the 2000 film, *O Brother, Where Art Thou?* Plenty of instruments and other artifacts are on display, but there's a lot more listening than looking here. You'll be given a set of headphones to carry around the museum and plug into various listening stations among the interactive exhibits.

You easily could spend hours here, enjoying the recorded music and interviews with Stanley. As it was, we stayed past closing time, but, as promised, no one ran us off.

Besides its mountain views and hiking trails, Breaks Interstate Park also has a peaceful lake and well-appointed cabins for rent.

the porch of our room sipping coffee, listening to the river rushing hundreds of feet below us, and watching the morning fog lift to reveal the sheer rock faces of the mountains across the gorge. Breakfast is served in the Rhododendron Restaurant in the park's visitor center, a wall of windows serving mountain scenes with plates filled with pancakes.

Besides hiking, we rent a pedal boat and tour the park's lake. The park also has a man-made pool and an outdoor amphitheater, cut into the side of a mountain—where a number of music festivals are held annually, including the Tri-State Gospel Sing every Labor Day weekend that attracts upwards of 20,000 visitors. I've attended one of those, and this much is true: The hills truly are alive with music. What could be more fitting on the Crooked Road?

IN THE AREA

Accommodations

FLOYD

Hotel Floyd, 120 Wilson Street, Floyd. Call 540-745-6080. Built in 2007 and designated as a "Virginia Green Lodging" establishment for its use of sustainable building materials and furnishings. Web site: http://www.hotelfloyd.com.

Mountain Rose Inn, 1787 Charity Highway, Woolwine. Call 276-930-1057. A 1901 Victorian home with private baths. Web site: http://www.mountainrose-inn.com.

INDEPENDENCE

Davis-Bourne Inn, 119 Journey's End Drive, Independence. Call 276-773-9384. A Victorian mansion from the 1860s that houses a bed-and-breakfast inn, as well as a restaurant. Web site: http://www.davisbourneinn.com.

Grayson Inn and Suites, 155 Rainbow Circle Drive, Independence. Call 276-773-3313. Good, basic motel in an area where there aren't many. Web site: http://www.grayson-inn.com.

DAMASCUS AND ABINGDON

Comfort Inn, 170 Jonesboro Road, Abingdon. Call 276-676-2222. Motel with continental breakfast. Web site: http://www.comfortinn.com.

Martha Washington Hotel and Spa, 150 W. Main Street, Abingdon. Call 276-628-3161. Historic upscale inn across from the Barter Theatre. Web site: http://www.marthawashingtoninn.com.

Mountain Laurel Inn, 22750 JEB Stuart Highway, Damascus. Call 276-475-5956. Country home built in the early 1900s. Web site: http://www.mountainlaurelinn.com.

BIG STONE GAP

Comfort Inn, 1928B Wildcat Road, Big Stone Gap. Call 276-523-5911. Lodge-like lobby lends the motel a rustic feel. Web site: http://www.comfortinn.com.

BREAKS INTERSTATE PARK

Rhododendron Lodge, Breaks Interstate Park, Breaks. Call 276-865-4413. Motel with a view. Park also has cabins and cottages. Web site: http://www.breakspark.com.

Attractions and Recreation

Barter Theatre, 127 W. Main Street, Abingdon. Call 276-628-3991. Year-round productions at the State Theatre of Virginia. Web site: http://www.bartertheatre.com.

Blue Ridge Institute and Museum, Ferrum College, Ferrum. Call 540-365-4416. A repository for documenting, interpreting, and presenting the folk heritage of the Blue Ridge. Web site: http://www.blueridgeinstitute.org.

Carter Family Fold, A. P. Carter Highway, Hiltons. Call 276-386-6054. Live music every Saturday night, museum, and store. Web site: http://www.carterfamilyfold.org.

Floyd Country Store, 206 S. Locust Street, Floyd. Call 540-745-4563. Old-style general store with live music on Friday nights and Sunday afternoons. Soups, sandwiches, homemade baked goods, and old-fashioned milk shakes. Web site: http://www.floydcountrystore.com.

Grayson Highlands State Park, 829 Grayson Highland Lane, Mouth of Wilson. Call 276-579-7092. Hiking, camping, and wild ponies in one of Virginia's most spectacular settings. Web site: http://www.dcr.virginia.gov/state_parks/gra.shtml.

Ralph Stanley Museum and Traditional Mountain Music Center, 249 Main Street, Clintwood. Call 276-926-8550. Tribute to Dickenson County native son and old-time mountain music star. Web site: http://www.ralphstanleymuseum.org.

Virginia Creeper Trail, Whitetop Station, Damascus, and Abingdon. A 34-mile biking and hiking trail. Web site: http://www.vacreepertrail.com.

Dining

Hillsville Diner, 525 N Main Street, Hillsville. Call 276-728-7681. True-blue diner serving breakfast and lunch. Closed Sunday.

Mosby's Restaurant, 251 Ridgeview Road, Wise. Call 276-679-0101. Wide-ranging menu served in a Civil War décor. Web site: http://www .mosbysrestaurant.com.

Oddfella's Cantina, 110A N. Locust Street, Floyd. Call 540-745-3463. Diverse menu featuring locally grown, seasonal products. Web site: http://www.oddfellascantina.com.

The Tavern, 222 E. Main Street, Abingdon. Call 276-628-1118. Constructed in 1779, the building is one of the oldest, west of the Blue Ridge. Used from the beginning as a tavern and overnight inn, The Tavern serves intercontinental cuisine in a casual setting. Closed Sunday. Web site: http://www.abingdontavern.com.

Tlaquepaque, 1003 E. Stuart Drive, Galax. Call 540-236-5060. Mexican restaurant with good food and fast service. Web site: http://www.planet-va.com/restaurants/Tlaquepaque.

Wildflour Bakery and Restaurant, 24443 Lee Highway, Abingdon. Call 276-676-4221. Good stop for morning coffee and freshly baked goods, but also later for lunch and dinner. Web site: http://www.facebook.com /pages/Abingdon-VA/Wildflour-Bakery-Cafe/252825453844?v=info.

Other Contacts

The Crooked Road: Virginia's Heritage Music Trail, 851 French Moore Jr. Boulevard, Suite 146, Abingdon. Call 276-492-2085. Information on maps, accommodations, and attractions along the route. Web site: http://www.thecrookedroad.org.

The road to Cumberland Gap carries the traveler through a gorgeous valley of pastures with mountain backdrops.

CHAPTER

19

Wilderness Road

Like Daniel Boone and other pioneers, heading to Cumberland Gap

Estimated length: 100 miles
Estimated time: 8 hours

Getting there: From Bristol, which is on I-81 and straddles the Virginia-Tennessee line, head west on US 58 to Cumberland Gap.

Highlights: Stopovers at **Natural Tunnel State Park** and **Wilderness Road State Park**, a scenic valley drive through the far southwestern corner of Virginia, and a visit to historic **Cumberland Gap** itself.

Daniel Boone, the legendary frontiersman, could be the patron saint for anyone who has done any traveling in unfamiliar settings, not only for blazing trails through the wilderness but for his wry reflection of it.

"I can't say as ever I was lost," he famously said, "but I was bewildered once for three days."

When I see that quotation posted in an exhibit at the visitor center at Natural Tunnel State Park, I do what I do every time I see or hear it. I smile, although I can't say I've been as fortunate as Boone, for I have been lost *and* bewildered, sometimes all at once.

Getting lost is still possible in this rural corner of Virginia, but not likely if you stick to US 58. The road roughly follows the last stretch of the old Wilderness Trail that Boone and his axmen fashioned, hacking through the forests and mountains to reach Cumberland Gap in 1775. Easy to navigate and often four lanes, US 58 presents far less of a challenge than what Boone faced when he was cutting through the steep, rough terrain, creating a gateway to the western frontier.

We make our way west from Bristol into a part of Virginia many Virginians never see. We will be 500 miles from the Atlantic coast by the time we reach Cumberland Gap, the westernmost point in Virginia that is as far west as Detroit. On previous trips here, I have met residents surprised and pleased to see someone from Richmond, their state capital.

"Most people think the state of Virginia ends at Exit 7," a man in the little community of Stickleyville told me, speaking of one of the I-81 exits in Bristol. "They say we're a suburb of Tennessee and Kentucky."

Indeed, at another stop on an earlier journey, folks living near Cumberland Gap introduced me as being from "Richmond, *Virginia.*" It seemed an odd reference until it dawned on me Richmond, *Kentucky,* is 350 miles closer than Richmond, *Virginia.* In their eyes, we truly were from a far-away region, if not another realm.

The **Cumberland Gap**, a rare break in the Appalachian Mountains, fueled the beginning of America's great migration west. In 1750, Dr. Thomas Walker, a surveyor, became the first white man to explore the Gap, which had been known to American Indians for generations as a route to western hunting grounds. However, his name takes a backseat in history—except in Virginia's **Lee County**, where a high school is named in his honor—to Daniel Boone who blazed a road to the Gap in 1775.

Soon, settlers seeking land and fresh starts flooded through this new gateway to the west. From 1780–1810, more than 200,000 people passed through the Gap to Kentucky and beyond. The Gap declined in importance in the later 1800s as canals, railroads, and better wagon roads crossed the Appalachians.

By the mid 1900s, a paved highway, US 25E, passed through the Gap, following the course of the original trail itself. Besides spoiling the historical spirit of the Gap, as well as its natural setting, the winding road was a motorist's nightmare and a frequent scene of accidents. With the completion of the Cumberland Gap Tunnel in 1996 and the removal of the old roadway, the restoration of the Gap is under way. Visitors can once again walk in the footsteps of Boone and see for themselves, up close, the famous V-notch in the mountains that opened the door to westward expansion.

Coal trains still run through Natural Tunnel.

The Daniel Boone Wilderness Trail, a self-guided driving tour with suggested stops along the way, stretches from Kingsport, Tennessee, to Cumberland Gap, a natural break in the mountains where Virginia, Kentucky, and Tennessee converge. We pick up the trail at Gate City, on US 58, and make our first stop, 15 miles later, at Natural Tunnel, declared the "eighth wonder of the world" by William Jennings Bryan. He might have moved it into the Top Five had the park's chairlift been around back then. The chairlift, when operating, makes it easy to travel from the visitor center down to the "floor" of the park and a 500-foot boardwalk that leads visitors to an up close view of the tunnel. A walking trail from the visitor center also goes to the tunnel.

Carved from limestone and bedrock by thousands of years of flowing water, the tunnel is 850 feet long and 100 feet high. Stock Creek runs through the tunnel. So does the railroad. Coal-carrying trains rumble through the tunnel several times a day; passenger trains stopped years ago. If you like loud noise, you'll love standing on the observation deck near the mouth of the tunnel as a train comes through. And if you like feeling small, you'll love looking up at the 400-foot-high cliff walls, trees perched precariously along the edge.

Elsewhere in the park, find the Wilderness Road Blockhouse, a re-created structure representative of gathering places for pioneers headed to Cumberland Gap. The park also offers hiking trails, a swimming pool, and an amphitheater for live music.

Back to US 58, we head to Duffield, a small community with shopping and gas stations, and then on to Stickleyville and Dot. Yes, Dot.

Dot is a dot on the map and little more. My first time here, my companion and I saw the DOT sign that signals to motorists they have arrived. We thought we'd drive to the end of town, find the DOT sign for eastbound traffic, turn around and come back. Except we found no town. Just a convenience store, a few scattered homes, and a business or two. We never saw the other DOT sign—until we turned around, came back, and found it on the other side of the original sign. Hello and goodbye, back to back. Great fun. I've liked Dot ever since.

Little more than a crossroads, Dot once had its own post office, but it's long gone. Now, Dot is simply a wide spot in the road, a place to stop and get gas or a cold drink on your way to the Gap.

After Dot, we see a gleaming example of economic revitalization: a $100 million, high-security federal prison that means jobs and revenue in a region that has lost both in recent years. Just the same, we maintain a steady speed and don't stop.

Next up is Jonesville, a town of 1,000 residents and the county seat of Lee County, named for Light Horse Harry Lee, a Virginia governor and father of General Robert E. Lee. Jonesville has a few shops and a Confederate cemetery. Civil War reenactors gather every June for a reenactment of the 1864 Battle of Jonesville, which the Confederates won.

The road opens up as we head west from Jonesville, deeper into the Powell Valley, for the last 30 miles to the Gap. Tobacco fields and rolling,

Tobacco fields remain common sights along the Wilderness Road.

green pastureland set against a dramatic, seamless mountain backdrop make for as pretty a drive as you'll find anywhere.

Part of the appeal of this stretch of road is the bucolic nature of it and its lack of commercialization. The flip side: There aren't a lot of places to eat. An occasional diner in one of the small towns just off the main road could be an option. Steph and Andy's Pizza Plus in Rose Hill, part of a regional chain of nothing-fancy pizza restaurants, looks like a fine place for a bite to eat and is. It always helps to see a couple of state troopers dining at a place you're considering. I load up on pizza and salad.

But for a slightly different dining experience, check out The Dutch Treat Country Store, a small, Mennonite-run grocery and bakery with what more than one local tells me are the best sandwiches in the valley. They have interesting cheeses and Amish butter. The freshly baked breads and pastries are excellent, too. I highly recommend the pumpkin roll.

If you have time, sign up for a cave tour. Our small group gathers at the **Daniel Boone Visitor Information Center**, a couple of miles east of the main visitor center, just off US 58, near Cumberland Gap, Tennessee. Two knowledgeable and entertaining young park rangers will lead the way.

We walk into the restored Gap to reach the mouth of the cave, where the year-round temperature is 59 degrees. It's also always dark. We carry flashlights provided by the rangers. We spend two hours in the cave, moving from chamber to chamber and level to level. We see bats and salamanders. We duck a lot, passing through places with low clearances the rangers have given names like Tall Man's Misery. One long, steep set of steps is dubbed The Ultimate Thighmaster. Besides knowing what they're talking about, the rangers also are very good-humored.

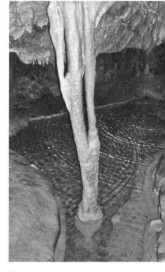

One also can sing. Lucas Wilder, who grew up in Ewing, breaks into song in the Music Room, a chamber with amazing acoustics. So, there we stand, in the dark, as Wilder sings, a capela, a haunting, country classic, "Long Black Veil." The cave is stone silent except for Wilder. Spellbound, no one else even breathes loudly.

A cave tour at Cumberland Gap takes visitors past Cleopatra's Pool and other natural attractions.

We see Cleopatra's Pool, a lovely, still reservoir, as well as quirky formations that look like fried eggs, strips of bacon, and the Pillar of Hercules, all the result of centuries of relentless dripping of mineral-laden water. Near the end of the tour, we find Civil War-era graffiti, soldiers having spent time in the cave, which, perhaps, was used in that era as a temporary hospital.

Walking through the cave is moderately strenuous, tight in spots, abruptly vertical in others, but no belly crawling is required. The footing is generally quite good, a walkway having been laid when the cave was a privately owned tourist attraction earlier in the 20th century.

But here's what I really like: the genuine enthusiasm and affection the rangers show for their work. When we're out of the cave, I ask Wilder about growing up in this part of the world. He loves this place, he says, and acknowledged he even sheds "a little tear" whenever he sees the WELCOME TO LEE COUNTY sign.

It means he's home.

"This is an amazing valley," says Sam Yoder, who operates The Dutch Treat and is a relative newcomer to the area. "There's so much history here."

Down the road, just past Ewing, we come to Wilderness Road State Park, behind a split-rail fence along US 58. Drive the park road behind the visitor center to find Martin's Station, a replica of a frontier fort that serves as a living-history museum. An 8-mile multipurpose trail, called the Wilderness Road Trail, bisects the park and connects it with the campground at Cumberland Gap National Historical Park. A small herd of bison roam a nearby pasture.

Virginia runs out before we get to the Gap, although the road doesn't. Staying on our same path, we cross briefly into Tennessee and then enter the Cumberland Gap Tunnel, which was built in the 1990s to replace the twisting, mountain road that actually followed the original Wilderness Trail along the edge of the mountain. The 4,600-foot tunnel goes through the mountain. When we come out the other end we are in Kentucky. Take the next exit to reach Cumberland Gap National Historical Park and the main visitor center.

To appreciate the history that came through here, you should spend some time viewing the exhibits and films at the center. For appreciation of another sort, visit the adjoining shop, Cumberland Crafts, which sells handmade crafts from the region. You will certainly want to drive the steep, twisting 4-mile-long Skyland Road to the Pinnacle Overlook, which affords a spectacular view of the three states. On the paved walkway leading to the observation deck, you can do something less dazzling but perhaps more satisfying: straddle two states. A painted white stripe marks the spot where Virginia and Kentucky meet. There's even a bench if you'd like to sit and savor the moment.

If you decide to stay the night, the nice little town of Cumberland Gap, Tennessee, just east of the tunnel, has several lodging options and a couple of restaurants, as well as a few shops. A few miles west of the tunnel, you'll find Middlesboro, Kentucky, which seemingly has every motel and restaurant chain known to man, and a Wal-Mart, too.

It's a far cry, of course, from the pioneer days. But before you go, take the time to stand in the restored Gap, gaze off in the distance and then down at your feet, knowing you're walking in the footsteps of Daniel Boone and hundreds of thousands of others who traveled the same path as they headed west to build America.

"This," a park ranger told me, "is ground zero for history."

IN THE AREA

Accommodations

Cumberland Gap Inn, 630 Brooklyn Street, Cumberland Gap, TN. Call 423-869-3996. Motel within walking distance of shops and attractions. Web site: http://www.cumberlandgap.net/inn/index.htm.

Estillville Bed & Breakfast, 128 Park Street, Gate City. Call 276-690-2091. An early 1900s home that was renovated and turned into an inn. Web site: http://www.gatecityinn.com.

Olde Mill Bed & Breakfast, 603 Pennlyn Street, Cumberland Gap, TN. Call 423-869-0868. An 1889 mill and 1750s cabin make this a historic place to sleep. Web site: http://www.oldemillinnbnb.com.

Attractions and Recreation

Cumberland Gap National Historical Park, US25E South, Middlesboro, KY. Call 606-248-2817. History, hiking, camping. cave tours. Web site: http://www.nps.gov/cuga.

Natural Tunnel State Park, 1420 Natural Tunnel Parkway, Duffield. Call 276-940-2674. Hiking, chairlift to tunnel, amphitheater, camping, and cabins. Web site: http://www.dcr.virginia.gov/state_parks/nat.shtml.

Wilderness Road State Park, Route 2, Box 115, Ewing. Call 276-445-3065. History, hiking, biking, picnicking. Primitive group camping available. Web site: http://www.dcr.virginia.gov/state_parks/wil.shtml.

Dining

Campus Drive-In, 184 Kane Street, Gate City. Call 276-386-3702. Burgers, fries, onion rings. Local institution.

Steph and Andy's Pizza Plus, Rural Route 1, Box 121, Rose Hill. Call 276-445-5701. Pizza, pasta, salad. Web site: http://www.pizzaplusinc.com.

The Dutch Treat Country Store, Route 2, Box 167, Rose Hill. Sandwiches, baked goods, hams, and jams.

Webb's Country Kitchen, 527 Colwyn Street, Cumberland Gap, TN. Call 423-869-5877. Southern cooking for breakfast, lunch, and dinner. Web site: http://www.cumberlandgap.net/Webbs/index.htm.

Other Contacts

Daniel Boone Wilderness Trail. Maps, attractions, links. Web site: http://www.danielboonetrail.com.

Middlesboro, Kentucky. Web site: http://www.middlesboroky.com.